Welcome

Welcome to **Let's Go Sea Fishing.**

Sea angling is all about having fun and catching fish for the whole family. There are many myths surrounding sea fishing suggesting that it is complicated and that the fish are hard to catch – well the truth is that it isn't at all difficult and the fish are easily caught when you know how.

To help you get under way and into this wonderful sport, this publication has been specially presented and packed with all you need to know about how to get going with confidence. You will learn how to target the core species in our waters and on what baits, as well as how to cast and to tie your own knots and rigs, along with much more!

I started sea fishing when I was just five years old – with my father on his boat, a small Mirror dinghy, off the Welsh and Scottish coasts during the summer holidays. We would go out maybe a few hundred yards and, generally, I would troll a set of mackerel feathers behind the boat, or drift fish with bait or lures. We always bagged up with mackerel when fishing the first me but were not so successful with the second. The areas we fished were hotspots and they still are to this day, but I still cringe at the opportunities we missed simply because we really had no idea of what we were doing – if only I'd had a sea fishing magazine to guide me back then!

Every month we produce Total Sea Fishing, a magazine full of information, tips, tricks and secrets. This publication is the perfect companion to that magazine and is crammed full of the skills you need to learn – whether you're a novice or expert, this publication will teach you the fundamentals as well as the more advanced skills you'll need to progress to the next level.

Whichever level you're at, you can be assured that if you love your sea fishing you will gain plenty from this publication! I hope you enjoy this read as much as we have putting it together. There's no time to waste – Let's Go Sea Fishing!

Barney

Published by David Hall Publishing Ltd. The advertisements and editorial content of this publication are the copyright of David Hall Publishing Ltd and may not be quoted, copied or reproduced without prior permission of the publisher.

Copyright © 2011
Edited by Barney Wright
Designed by Rebecca Abbott
Reprographics by Derek Mooney, Steph Horn and Adam Mason
Sub edited by Dean Kirkman

Contents

Bait

08 Dig Your Own *Lugworms*
18 How To Find And Use *Peeler Crabs*
28 Dig Your Own *Ragworms*
40 How To Use *Bluey*
48 Collect And Use *Mussels*
58 How To Use *Mackerel*
68 How To Use *Razorfish*
98 How To Use *Sandeels*

Shore Fishing

Catch More…
04 Surf *Cod*
14 Surf *Bass*
24 Estuary *Flounders*
44 Rough-Ground *Cod*
54 *Whiting*
64 *Dabs*
79 *Thornback Rays*
95 *Plaice*
103 *Mullet*

Boat Fishing

Catch More…
36 *Smoothhounds*
86 *Pollack*
109 *Tope*

Rigs

How to build and use…
10 The Two-Hook Seesaw Wishbone
20 The Elevator
30 The Three-Hook Flapper
42 The Pulley
50 The Northeast Rough-Ground Cod
60 The Three-Hook Clipped-Down
70 The Two-Hook Leger/Drift
84 The Two-Hook Cascade
100 The European Three-Hook Sweeper
112 The Shark Trace

Knots

How to tie and why…
09 The Uni Knot
19 The Shockleader
29 The Half Blood
41 Joining Two Running Lines
49 The Twisted Boom
59 The Stop Knot
69 The Spider Hitch Shockleader
73 The Albright
93 The Domhoff
99 The Rapala

Tackle & Skills

12 A Guide To Hooks
22 A Guide To Lures
27 Which Beach Rod?
32 Cast The Wright Way – Learn The Off-The-Ground Cast
52 Multiplier Braking Systems
72 Lubricating A Multiplier
74 Cast Bait Further – The Pendulum Cast
90 Kayak Safety
106 Clothing
114 Which Boat Rod?

Surf Cod

Cod are great fish to target, and here's how...

The cod is a distinctive-looking fish and can only really be confused with its near cousin the whiting. Comparing the two: the cod has a more blunt head shape, with the whiting's being more pointed. The lateral line on the cod is also more pronounced with an upward curve above the pectoral fin. The whiting also carries a definite black spot at the root of the pectoral fin, whereas the cod does not.

Cod range widely in colour. Over sand they're mottled fawn or brown on the back with white undersides, but those resident over mixed ground become a more mottled green on the back.

This past winter has seen anglers in some areas enjoy much better cod fishing than there has been for years. There are several reasons for this but, chiefly, cod have enjoyed good spawning conditions for two of the past five years, plus some areas of the sea have been closed to commercial fishing, which has benefited the amount of cod available.

Cod reach sexual maturity at four years old, and a female cod can produce as many as 10 million eggs. It wouldn't take them long to refill the seas if they were left alone to breed for a few years. Although the fry are rarely seen, by the end of their second spring they will be inshore in huge numbers, ranging from four to seven inches in size. At three years old a typical codling will weigh 4lb, but is still not fully mature.

They have big mouths and are eating machines, hoovering up worms, crabs, squat lobsters, shrimps, shellfish, small pout, poor cod, sprats, whiting, sandeels, flatfish and even cod. They're adaptive fish and will eat pretty much anything that's available.

When And Where To Fish

The winter cod season starts in early September in South Wales and along the northeast and northwest coasts. In late September it starts in East Anglia and along the southeast coast.

Catches tend to peak around Christmas because the fish stay inshore until late January.

Some areas experience a run of cod in spring. These include East Anglia, Yorkshire and Humberside, and to some extent the Cumbrian coast and, of late, South Wales. These are generally smaller codling up to 5lb that appear in mid-March and run through until early May.

Tackle

For clean and mixed rough ground cod fishing choose a 12ft to 13ft 6in beachcaster, ideally with a stiff and fast-taper action, that's capable of casting 5oz to 6oz of lead and bait.

For clean ground an ABU 6500 or Daiwa 7HT with 15lb line and a 60lb shockleader is fine, but for rougher ground and big seas the better option would be a Penn 525 loaded with 20lb line and 80lb shockleader.

How To Make A Clipped-Down Pennel Cod Rig

1 Start with a 30in length of 60lb rig-body line. Tie on a Gemini lead link at the base.

2 Slide on a Breakaway Impact Shield followed by a bead and crimp above it. Position the Impact Shield just above the link knot and secure the crimp in place, leaving about an inch for the Impact Shield to slide in.

3 Slide on a rig crimp, a rig bead, a small rig swivel, another bead and a crimp. Leave these loose for now.

4 To the remaining free end of a 60lb line add a strong size 4 rig-body swivel.

5 The hook trace is a 24in length of 40lb clear line. Fluorocarbon is good because it has a high resistance to abrasion,

plus it's a little stiffer than mono and less prone to tangling in high-surf conditions.

6 Use a two-hook Pennel rig incorporating a Viking 79510 for the top hook and a Viking 79515 for the lower hook, both 4/0s. The top hook is held in place by passing the line through the eye of the hook, sliding the line through a short length of rubber tubing, then passing the hook point through the tubing so that the tubing sits tight on the shank of the hook, then tie on the second hook below.

7 Put the bottom hook in the clip of the Impact Shield and slide the rig, bead and swivel assembly up the trace until the hooklength comes just tight, then secure the rig crimps in place.

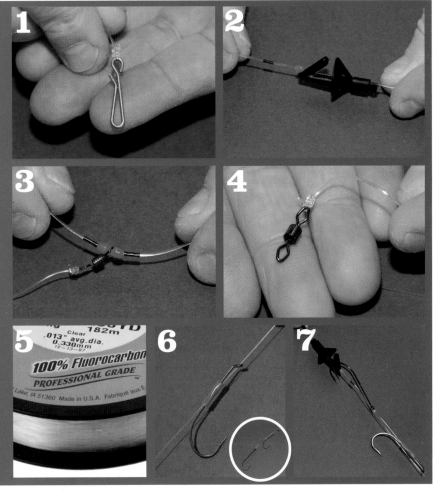

10 TopTips For Cod

1 Check out rougher ground and don't be afraid of tackle losses because this is where the cod will be hunting crabs and small fish such as gobies and small wrasse. Areas of rough ground also catch and hold food that's washed down with the tide over clean sand – they're real hotspots, however small. Identifying such areas can often mean the difference between catching some cod and blanking!

2 When deliberately casting into rough ground, tackle losses can be minimised by swapping the stiff wire used on most grip leads for softer, bendable wires. Make these long, up to four inches higher than the lead body, so that they sit on the rocks and boulders meaning that the lead is less likely to slip down between the rocks. These soft wires will still grip well, but are easier to pull out when direct pressure is applied via the line if the grips snag.

3 If you have a strong lateral tide run, say from left to right, then casting straight out from your actual fishing station will see you end up, when the line is tightened to the lead, with a big bow of line heading off to the right, which ruins bite detection and can cause the lead weight to skip free due to tide pressure.

To combat this, walk in an uptide direction, in this case to the left, around 40 yards then cast out as normal. Walk back to your rod rest, winding in line as you go, then, as you reach your base camp and the line comes tight to the lead, when you put the rod in the rest you'll see that the line faces straight out to sea with no bow.

You can still do this if you have anglers to the side of you providing you can outcast them. You'll only snag them if you're casting closer in than they are.

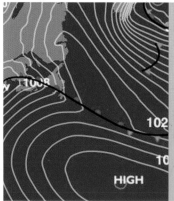

4 Watch for major weather depressions across the Atlantic. These bring gales and rough seas to both the west-facing and east-facing coasts of the UK. The wind initially blows hard from the southwest then, as the barometric pressure rises, the wind swings northeast. Although the wind eases as the gales pass through, the sea is rough, well coloured and full of stirred-up food that brings the cod tight in to the shore to feed.

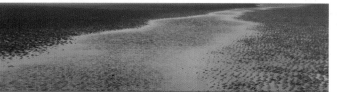

5 The military says: "Time spent in reconnaissance is never wasted!" Well this is good advice. Check the venue that you aim to fish at low water and note the features. You're looking for deeper gutters and gullies that run in line with the beach, deeper areas where the tide drains off the beach, and patches of stones, weed and coarse gravel. Cod also like to work through small groups of stones that occur scattered among the sand. Anything that breaks up the monotony of sand is worth a cast!

6 During prolonged rough seas, large amounts of shellfish – usually found a little way offshore such as big mussels, queen cockles, razorfish and sand clams – become washed up and smashed on the beach. When this occurs the cod can go into a feeding frenzy. At such times, simply tipping your normal lug baits with any of these shellfish can double your catch. Razorfish is particularly effective!

7 Good all-round cod baits are obviously blow and black lug, mussels – which even work over sand – razorfish and squid, with peeler crabs the top spring bait especially when fishing into or among rocky ground. Fish baits are poor in comparison, though bluey, with its high oil content, does seem to catch cod far better than mackerel or herring will, so is well worth carrying.

8 If you choose to fish a beach with wooden groynes at the top, it's a sure indication that it will fish best for three hours either side of low water. Cod, and many other fish, will not usually venture in between the groynes because the tide flow is minimal and food is not displaced readily here. Long-range casters who can fish past the groyne ends may still catch over high water, but if you can't, don't waste time. Move to another venue where groynes are not a feature.

9 Where possible, always fish two rods, ideally identical rods. Big cod can often take a bait and give slow slack line that is easy to miss on the rod tip. Two identical rods side by side mean that you have improved bite detection because both rods behave the same with the tips pulled slightly over until a bite occurs. Two rods also allow you to fish one bait at maximum range and the other at medium range until the fish are found, then you can fish both rods at the same distance to maximise your catch. Using two rods also gives you the opportunity to fish two different baits, or bait combos, to find out what the cod want best on the night.

10 Even though the sea will be well coloured, invariably the best of the fishing will be through the hours of darkness. Try to time your fishing with the tides where low water and the full flood tide falls in darkness. When low water occurs during daylight, this can restrict the amount of cod that move inshore during that tide, especially if the venue you're fishing is shallow with water less than eight feet in depth, such as a western surf beach.

'SUPER TUNED' TO UP YOUR GAME.

Dig Your Own
Lugworms

It not only saves you money but it's great exercise too!

The first thing you need to do is find an area with plenty of lug casts, either on an open beach or in an estuary. As the tide recedes, the worms make their casts but the sand will still be holding a lot of water, so initially you need to dig a horseshoe-shaped trench in order to drain the water. You'll start finding worms as you dig the trench, and when you've finished digging the horseshoe, leave it for a few minutes to let all the water drain away. Start digging at the top of the horseshoe where the sand is dry and much easier to dig and continue until you've dug the whole patch. You may get a bonus of white rag and maddies

as you dig; you can either tip the lug with these or use them at slack water for scratching out small fish such as dabs, pout and rockling.

If you're digging individual worms, look for the cast and the blowhole; the worm will be nearer the cast so start digging near the blowhole to remove the bulk of the sand.

Begin by digging down half the depth of the tines of your fork, then take another dig a few inches back to their full depth to remove the bulk of the sand. Finally, your last dig will be just behind the cast and down to the full fork depth again; carefully lift the sand out and your worm should be in this last forkful.

TopTips

1 When you've finished digging, lay the worms on clean, dry newspaper and pick out any lumps of mud, sand and shell. Then wrap them loosely in the paper and store in a fridge until you're ready to fish. Check them daily and remove any dead or damaged worms. Renew the paper every two days and your worms should stay in good condition for up to a week.

2 As a bonus, white rag and maddies often come up with the lug

The Tool And The Groundwork

1 A fork with wide tines will lift sand and mud better than a garden fork.

2 Select an area with plenty of worm casts and dig a horseshoe-shaped trench to drain off water.

3 When the water has drained to the lower end of the trench, start digging the dry sand at the top.

The Close-In Technique

1 If you're digging individual worms, identify the cast and the blowhole before you start digging.

2 Start at the blowhole and remove one or two forkfuls of sand; the last dig should be behind the cast where the worm will be lying.

3 The prize – a big, fat, juicy lugworm for your bait collection.

The Uni Knot

Learn how to tie the perfect uni knot with this simple step-by-step guide.

Knowing your knots is essential for fishing, yet still so many are tied incorrectly. They join our lines, secure our hooks, leads and swivels and are what keeps our gear together as we cast out and catch fish.

Some knots are complicated and some simple but all have their applications. Knowing which knot to use and when is also the key to catching your target species – and knowing how to tie them properly is an absolute must.

The uni knot has several uses, but the most common one is attaching line to a hook, swivel or link. Follow our step-by-step guide and learn how to tie the perfect uni knot.

TopTips

1 The uni knot is excellent for tying hooks when using worm baits, because the tag points up and will help to snag the worm and stop it from sliding down.

2 The knot tightens with use and will not come loose.

3 Thin lines such as 10lb ones need five or six turns in the loop, but three or four turns are ample for 50lb lines.

4 For extra strength you can pass the line through the hook eye twice before making the knot.

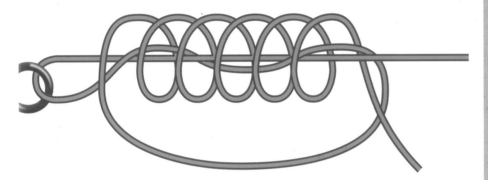

How To Tie The Uni Knot

1 Pass the line through the eye of the hook and allow an 8in tag end. Make three or four turns with the tag and the main line.

2 Form a loop as shown, then pass the tag end through the big loop four to five times in the same direction as the first turn.

3 Now lubricate with saliva and gently pull on the tag end to make the coils come together – but don't tighten yet.

4 Coax the coils together using your thumb and forefinger so that they are snug, but still not tight. Pull on the tag to assist.

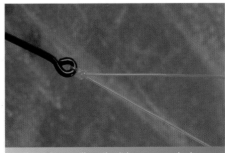

5 The knot will easily slide up towards the hook eye, but lubricate again if necessary. Now pull it tight with a firm but steady pull.

6 The coils will tighten down at this point, then you can trim the tag. You should have a perfect knot that looks like this.

Two-Hook Seesaw Wishbone RIG

History Of The Rig

You have to go back to the late 19th/early 20th century to find the forerunners of the modern seesaw wishbone rig. Our forefathers back then were using V-shaped brass-wire spreaders with an eye formed in the middle and round eyes formed in the ends of the wire. The main line went to the middle eye, with the short gut hook links attached to the leg eyes. This was designed to keep two baits side by side but without tangling.

It wasn't until the early 1970s, a time of great revolution in sea angling, that the idea of having a wishbone-type rig gained favour again. Initial rigs were just a length of mono with a loop tied in one end to create the two hook links, but this was prone to tangling. Beads were used pushed up tight against the knot and held in place with stop knots to act as a spreader bar, which was okay for short to medium-range casting, but then the idea progressed to having a single length of line running through a swivel eye with beads and stop knots or crimps, allowing the lengths of hook links to be varied.

This was the breakthrough and the rig then went on to become a classic competition rig for small species, but was also adapted by freelance anglers who realised its potential for plaice and especially smaller shoal fish that have to compete for food.

How It Works

The key to the success of this rig is that you have two baits lying close together. This offers several advantages. Firstly, having two small baits near to each other means that you are putting the same amount of scent into the water as one big bait would, but with the advantage that the two smaller baits can be presented on small hooks to catch the smaller fish that happen along.

The other side of the coin is that the large amount of scent from two baits will draw bigger fish in that can still be caught on the small hooks, plus fish will often swallow both baits in one gulp, giving a double hook-hold.

Some anglers use a bigger bait on a size 3/0 hook on one side, but a small chunk of the same bait on a smaller size 2 to 4 Aberdeen alongside. They're working on the illusion that a small bit of bait has broken free of the main lump and is giving a more natural appearance. Anglers using this method will agree that the small bait does get taken more frequently than the bigger piece, and often by decent-sized fish that are well capable of swallowing the bigger bait just as easily.

By sliding the rubber rig stops to different positions above the hook, you can fish one hook on a shorter trace and the other on a longer trace to vary presentation. This works well when choosing a combination such as a section of peeler crab on the short link as a high-scent bait designed to initially attract the fish from long range downtide, but with the longer link carrying ragworm that moves in the tide to naturally draw the fish's eye as it approaches.

For the matchman and the keen freelancer, using two hooks side by side also means that you can better experiment with baits to find the best taker on the day.

1 Take a 42in length of 60lb rig-body line. At the base, tie on a Gemini lead and bait-clip link.

2 Add a rig crimp, followed by a rig bead, a size 6 rig swivel then another bead and a crimp. Be sure to leave these loose for now.

3 Tie on a size 4 rig-body connector swivel as the rig-to-leader connector.

4 Take two feet of 60lb rig-body line and tie this to the size 6 rig swivel. This heavier, stiffer line will minimise tangles. Tie another size 6 rig swivel to the end of this 60lb line.

5 The hook link needs to be 25lb, ideally fluoro, but mono is okay, and about 26 inches long. Tie a size 2 Aberdeen hook at one end, slide on a sequin and a rubber rig stop.

6 Pass the free end of the line through the free eye of the swivel tied to the 60lb line, then add another rubber rig stop, a sequin and tie on another hook. The rubber rig stops act as a sliding stop only, allowing the line to seesaw only so far before the rig stop jams up against the eye of the swivel. Some prefer to fish the hook trace as shown to provide one long hooklength, and the other very short, plus it minimises tangles. If you want to equalise each hooklength either side of the swivel, add another rig stop on each side above the first rig stop to act as a sliding adjuster.

7 Finish the rig by putting the hooks in the lead and bait-clip link, then slide the main hook-snood swivel up the rig body until the hook snood comes just tight. Now crimp everything in place.

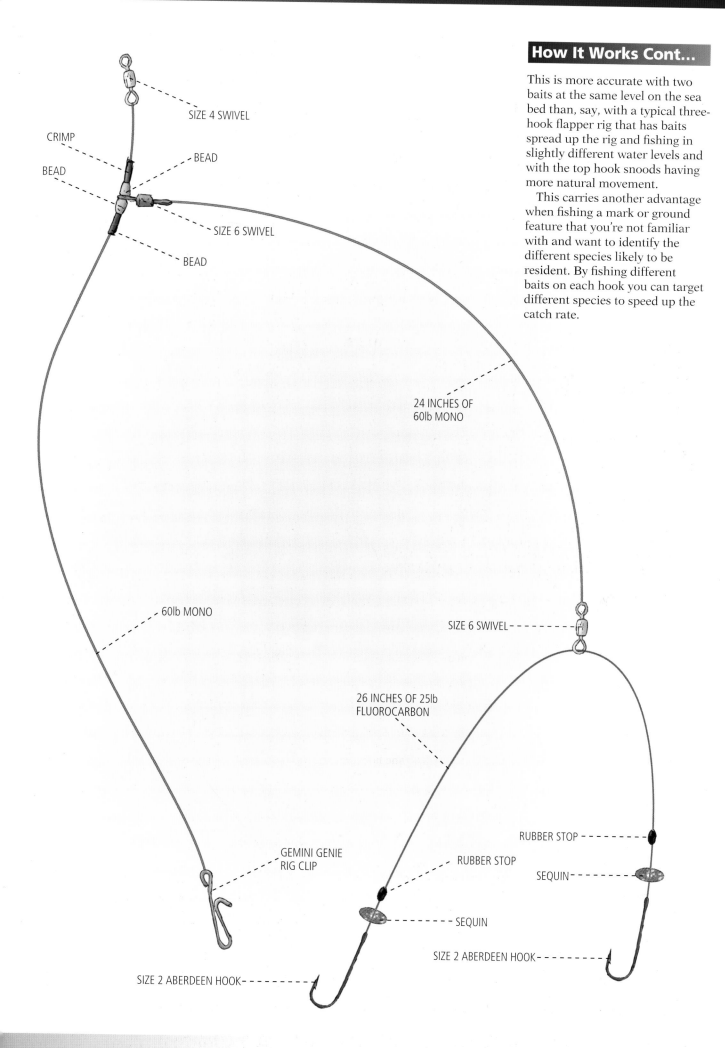

SIZE 4 SWIVEL

CRIMP

BEAD

BEAD

SIZE 6 SWIVEL

BEAD

This is more accurate with two baits at the same level on the sea bed than, say, with a typical three-hook flapper rig that has baits spread up the rig and fishing in slightly different water levels and with the top hook snoods having more natural movement.

This carries another advantage when fishing a mark or ground feature that you're not familiar with and want to identify the different species likely to be resident. By fishing different baits on each hook you can target different species to speed up the catch rate.

24 INCHES OF
60lb MONO

60lb MONO

SIZE 6 SWIVEL

26 INCHES OF 25lb
FLUOROCARBON

RUBBER STOP

SEQUIN

GEMINI GENIE
RIG CLIP

RUBBER STOP

SEQUIN

SIZE 2 ABERDEEN HOOK

SIZE 2 ABERDEEN HOOK

SIZE 2 ABERDEEN HOOK

Guide To Hooks

Know which hook to use for the bait you're using and the fish you're after.

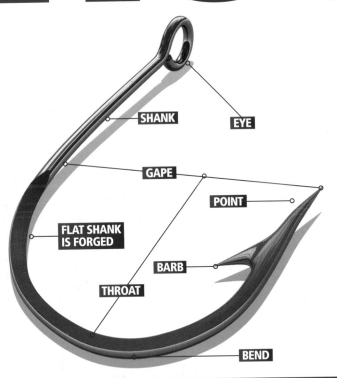

SHANK
EYE
GAPE
POINT
FLAT SHANK IS FORGED
BARB
THROAT
BEND

Fish hooks have been around for thousands of years. Some of the earliest types of hook recorded can be dated to around 7,000BC. Man has made fish hooks from all kinds of materials, including wood, animal and human bone, horn, stone, bronze and iron, plus modern materials like carbon steel.

Many anglers become obsessed with having the right rod and reel or line but often overlook the importance of hooks. Let's face it, you can have the best rod, reel and line in the world but if there's no hook on the end to snag your prey, the rest is useless. In many cases you don't even need a rod and reel… just line and a hook!

Hooks come in all shapes and sizes, from a size 4 fine-wire to target flatfish, up to mighty 20/0 forged hooks for large sharks. These many different sizes and styles of hook are all designed to present a bait or lure to attract a fish – then hook it so you can pull it in.

Hook Guide

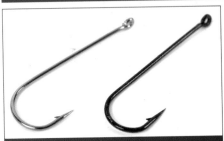

1 The long-shanked Aberdeen is one of the most popular patterns for many species, from whiting to flatfish.

2 The O'Shaughnessy pattern is a very strong hook and is popular for larger species, such as congers and skate.

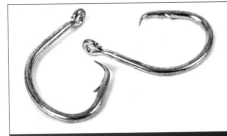

3 Circle hooks are becoming more popular because they almost always hook a fish in the corner of the mouth, meaning that the fish can be returned unharmed.

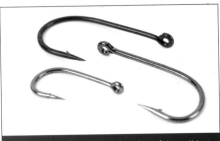

4 Short-shanked hooks are ideal for small baits such as crabs, and for species like bream, mullet and garfish.

5 Treble hooks are generally fitted on many types of lure – especially plugs.

6 A blunt hook is useless, so get yourself a hook-sharpening stone or a diamond hook sharpener to keep your hooks needle sharp.

Surf Bass

Get your tackle ready for a **surf-bass** session as we show you when, where and how to catch more.

Bass are distinctive fish, having two dorsal fins; the front carries eight to nine sharp spines and the body is covered in big scales. The coloration tends to be green grey on the back, occasionally dark blue, shading to silver sides and a white belly. Some sport a dark spot on the gill cover. Only the black bream looks remotely similar but it is far more oval, while the bass is a long, round-bodied fish.

Bass range as far south as the Mediterranean and the North African coast and north to southern Norway. They are common throughout the southern half of the UK, but during the past 15 years they have extended their range along the east and west coasts of Scotland and are now caught as far north as Dunnet and occasionally from the beaches on the Orkney Islands. Bass are also commonly found along the southeast, southern and southwestern coasts of Ireland and, to a lesser extent, along the north coast of Northern Ireland.

They have a wide-ranging diet, taking crabs, shellfish, shrimps, sandeels, worms and small fish such as gobies, blennies, pouting, poor cod, rockling, sprats and squid, and will often scavenge human food waste, such as bacon and chicken bones, inside harbours.

Their breeding season is from late January through to late May and generally occurs in deeper water offshore. Some knowledgeable bass anglers have, however, witnessed large adult bass behaving in a breeding manner in shallow water at the heads of estuaries in the mid-May period.

Where And When

Bass can be caught throughout the year south of a line drawn between Cumbria and North Yorkshire, but in the far north of Scotland the season tends to be late June through to late October. In southern Ireland bass can be caught all year round, especially in Wexford, Cork and Kerry but in the north the season is shortened, from mid-June through to late October.

The best of the surf-bass beaches tend to be shallow, often cut with parallel deeper gutters, and will fully or partially face the prevailing winds. Ideal surf conditions, produced by steady force 2 to force 5 onshore winds, tend to be when the surf tables are wide and not when the surf is short and breaking close together.

In a good surf and coloured water, bass can be caught in

How To Build A Surf-Bass Rig

1 Begin with about 30 inches of clear mono. Tie a Gemini lead link to one end.

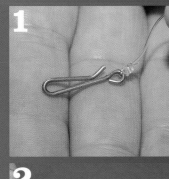

2 Slide on a Breakaway Impact Shield followed by a 3mm bead and a rig crimp. Crimp the Shield in place two inches above the lead link.

3 Now slide on a rig crimp, a 3mm bead, a size 10 rolling swivel, another bead and a crimp. Leave these loose for now. Tie on a size 4 rolling swivel to the free end of the 60lb line.

4 To the hook-trace swivel tie on 20 inches of 30lb fluorocarbon line or clear mono. Slide on a 5mm bead and add a single size 2/0 Mustad Viking 79515 hook.

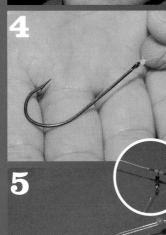

5 Position the Impact Shield just above the lead link and put the hook inside the clip of the lead link. Slide the hook-trace swivel and crimp assembly up the rig body until the trace becomes tight...

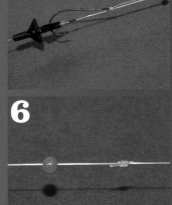

6 ... then crimp the snood swivel in place. Above the 5mm bead, tie on a stop knot of 14lb Powergum to act as a bait stop.

daylight, but the best of the fishing will generally be during the hours of darkness.

Tides are important. Bass tend to work a beach from low water and for the first two hours, then typically disappear for the middle hours of the flood, returning for the final hour before high water and sometimes staying for the first hour of the ebb. This is a general rule, but some beaches can produce bass down the ebb and rarely on the flood. This scenario often occurs when an estuary flanks the beach. The bass run the estuary on the flood but drop back down the length of the beach with the ebbing tide.

Always look for fish-holding features. These will be deeper gutters, especially if they have loose stones and pebbles in, because these hold food. Other features, such as single big stones or small sandbanks, will also attract fish.

There's an old adage that the bass are behind the third breaker, but this generally isn't true. Bass can be at your feet or 150 yards or more out. Typically, in ideal surf conditions and depending on depth, the bass will be from 20 to 80 yards out but often working a precise band of water a set distance offshore. This will change as water deepens and shallows with the tide.

In really rough seas big bass may again be very close in among the breakers, but they are more likely to be 100 yards or more out in the deeper water where the undertow from the surf pulls food back out – dislodging it from the sand.

Tackle

A surf rod would be rated 2oz to 4oz and be between 11ft 6in and 11ft 9in for surf bass. The action needs to be a semi-supple tip, but with quickening power in the upper mid section to drive hooks home at long range.

Top reels to go with this type of rod would be the ABU 5500 C3 CT and the 6500 C3 CT, which have been classic surf-bass reels for several decades due to their casting ability with lighter leads. If you prefer a fixed-spool reel, look at an 060 or 070-sized version holding 300 yards of 15lb line. Good examples are the Penn Sargus and the Shimano Navi.

Leads are typically 2oz to 4oz and should be grip wires in normal surf conditions. You can use a plain lead and let the tide wash this around in a semicircle back to shore to cover more ground, but choose a lead heavy enough to only move slowly across the sand due to tidal pressure on the line.

Bait

Lugworms are arguably the most consistent bass bait in the surf. Then it's sandeels, followed by ragworms and peeler crabs. Razorfish can be deadly after storms, and in autumn bigger bass will also take mackerel heads, whole squid and half-body sections of blueys.

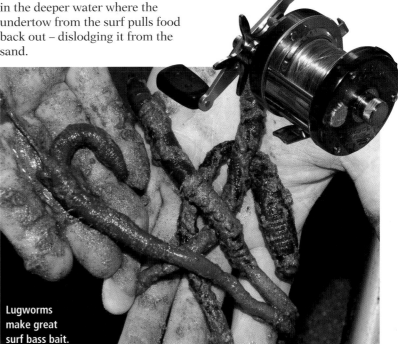

Lugworms make great surf bass bait.

5 TopTips For Bass

1 Look for areas where the surf breaks closer in along the surf line. This indicates deeper water behind it where food will collect. In heavy surf conditions look for areas where the surf tables are longest in between the breakers. Here the water is steadier and more predictable, and the bass will feed here.

2 You'll hit more bass bites if you hold the rod all the time and feel for bites to gain a quicker reaction time. Face the sea slightly sideways on and hold the rod across the body with the rod tip parallel to the surf, the tip pointing slightly down and the line tight to the lead.

4 Fluorocarbon is the better hook-trace material, even at night, because it's slightly stiffer than monofilament of the same breaking strain and tangles less in the surf. In daylight, it's also less visible than the mono when fishing in shallow, calmer water.

3 Bass take bait in the surf when swimming forwards. The bite will typically be a sudden hard pull down on the rod tip as the fish pulls the grip lead free from the sand. As this happens, instantly strike by rapidly lifting the rod tip in a high upwards arc away from the direct line to the fish.

5 Don't make your baits too big. Use two medium-sized blow lug up the hook, then lay another lug underneath these and whip the lot together with bait elastic. This is plenty big enough to take big bass, but can also be cast to maximum distance with a lighter 3oz lead when necessary.

Find Your Own
Peeler Crabs

How to collect and prepare peelers for the hook.

As crabs get bigger they have to grow new skin, shedding their old hard shells. Once the shells are discarded they become vulnerable to attack from other crabs and fish, so hide away under rocks and seaweed until their new skin hardens. The crabs start peeling in the spring, around April or May, when the water temperature reaches about 10 degrees, and may peel two to three times during the spring and summer months until the temperature drops in the autumn.

Where

Peeling shore crabs can be found at low tide under weed-covered boulders, groynes and pier piles. It can be difficult to tell a peeler from a hard crab; sometimes you can tell just by looking at one because the shell can be dull and may be starting to crack and lift. A sure method is to remove the last segment of the rear leg by gently twisting and pulling it off.

If it's a peeler the hard shell will be empty and you'll see the new fleshy segment exposed.

Once you've collected a few peelers, keep them cool in a bucket covered in wet seaweed then transfer them to your bait fridge. You can store them in cat-litter trays covered in seaweed and they'll keep for several days but you must keep them cool and check them daily – removing any dead crabs immediately.

Preparation

To prepare a crab for bait you must remove all the hard shell, removing the legs first then the belly and back shell. They can be used whole for cod, bass and smoothhounds, or cut into pieces for small species or to tip off worm baits. Once you have a crab on the hook you'll need to secure it in place with fine bait elastic, because a fish will soon rip off the soft flesh.

Peelers can be found under weed-covered rocks.

How To Bait Up With Peeler Crab

1 If the shell is starting to lift, it's a peeler!

2 Another way to check is to remove the end section of the back leg to reveal the new and soft leg underneath.

3 Take off all the legs and claws, then all of the hard shell.

4 Once you've got rid of all the hard shell, cut the crab in half…

5 … and stitch the hook through the soft flesh as many times as you can.

6 Finally, secure the crab with bait elastic.

The Shockleader Knot

Learn how to tie a leader knot, which is an essential safety aspect of all beachcasting.

There are immense forces at work during a cast, which put the line through extremely high stress. The purpose of a shockleader is to absorb the shock from the cast and reduce the chances of the line snapping. For this purpose we use between 60lb and 80lb monofilament, which is tied direct to the running line.

This heavy line will absorb the casting forces and allow you to send bait safely as far as you are able. There is a rule that states: "The lighter the lead, the lighter the leader can be." For example,

start at 50lb breaking strain for a 4oz sinker and add 10lb for every ounce extra over this. But the truth is, why not use 80lb for all general beach fishing? Then there can be no mistakes.

The leader material can also readily handle the abrasive actions of sand, rocks and shingle, which is important because it is this line that mostly comes into contact with these objects.

The use of a leader knot will improve your confidence in casting and fishing, because concerns of the line breaking will not be an issue.

TopTips

1 Use saliva to lubricate the knot when tightening.

2 Make sure you have at least eight turns of leader line around the multiplier spool, or four for a fixed-spool reel.

3 Make the leader a minimum of one-and-a-half times the length of the rod you are using.

4 Try to trim the tag ends as tight as possible so that they don't catch the rings or snag on the spool.

How To Tie A Shockleader Knot

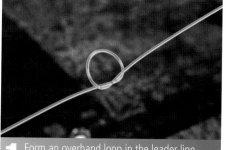

1 Form an overhand loop in the leader line with plenty of tag.

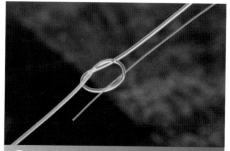

2 Pass the running line a few inches through the loop that you've formed and in the direction pictured.

3 Pull the overhand loop as tight as you can, lubricate, then pull the running line through as this part will be slightly crushed and damaged.

4 Form a uni-knot with the running line, lubricate, pull up until nearly tight and bunch up the coils formed.

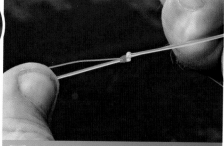

5 Moisten with saliva, slide the two knots together, then make a firm and steady pull. This tightens the whole knot down.

6 Trim the tag ends close and it's job done!

The Elevator RIG

History Of The Rig

No-one is really sure about where the concept for this rig originated. Anglers in Wales, Hampshire, East Anglia and on the northeast coast all lay claim to it, although a couple of Scottish shore match anglers were using a rig not too dissimilar to the original quite a few years ago, but they kept it quiet.

It's called the 'elevator rig' because the hook trace moves up and down. When casting, the trace is positioned where a normal clipped-down rig would be, but when being fished it is able to slide down to the lead.

The original rig used a loop of line to hold the Cascade swivel in place but that never looked completely right, so this alternative system was devised to fish much better and reduce the clutter when constructing the rig.

How It Works

When set up, the rig works like a normal clipped-down paternoster and is capable of being cast to maximum range because it's streamlined with the bait directly behind the lead. As the lead hits the water, the line pressure falls slack, the inverted Gemini link flips up and the hook trace releases naturally. As the rig falls through the water column, the water pressure means that the trace remains at the top of the rig. But as the lead hits the sea bed, gravity and tidal pressure mean that the hook trace slides down the rig to fish the bait hard on the sea bed, flowing-trace style.

By using a Sakuma sliding rig crimp above the bait shield the hook trace can be replaced should it become damaged during fishing. It also makes it easy to adjust the bait-shield position without being too precise about the new trace length. To prevent the hook trace stretching during powerful casting it's also best to have the bait shield sliding a little.

It is important to use a quality three-way rolling swivel. Do not confuse these with cheaper barrel swivels, which do not have the strength for maximum power casting. However, rolling swivels do have the strength and can be cast with confidence.

Built as shown, the rig can be used for long-range beach fishing for rays and turbot, and in deeper-water situations at long range for bass, cod and huss.

You can reduce the breaking strain of the hook trace to 20lb and drop the hook to a size 2 Aberdeen pattern to target flatfish, gurnards and codling off beaches and rock ledges – also piers, jetties and harbour walls when long casts are needed.

This rig can also be used for uptide fishing off the boat when targeting rays, smoothhounds, bass, cod and big flatfish with great success. In fact, it's become a very well used and reliable rig!

Build Sequence

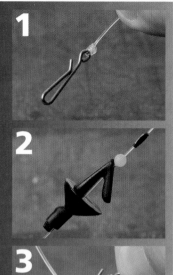

1 Take 42 inches of 60lb clear mono. At one end, tie on a Gemini lead link.

2 Slide on a Breakaway Impact Shield followed by a 5mm bead, a Sakuma sliding rig crimp and another 5mm bead.

3 Slide on a Breakaway Cascade swivel via the large eye.

4 Finish the main rig by tying on a strong size 4, three-way rolling swivel.

5 To the middle eye of the three-way swivel, clip on a Gemini lead link, which will sit inverted.

6 The hook trace is 30 inches of 40lb fluorocarbon or clear mono. Finish the hook trace by sliding on a 5mm bead and tie on a Mustad Viking 79515 hook, size 3/0 or 4/0 for rays and cod.

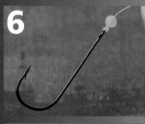

7 Above the hook, tie on a Powergum stop knot to hold the bead in place and act as a bait stop.

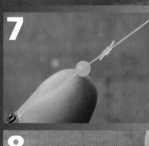

8 Place the hook in the bait shield, slide the Breakaway Cascade swivel up the rig body and clip it into the inverted Gemini link. Hold this in position as you slide the bait clip and hook downwards to set the correct tension for casting, so the hook remains set in the shield.

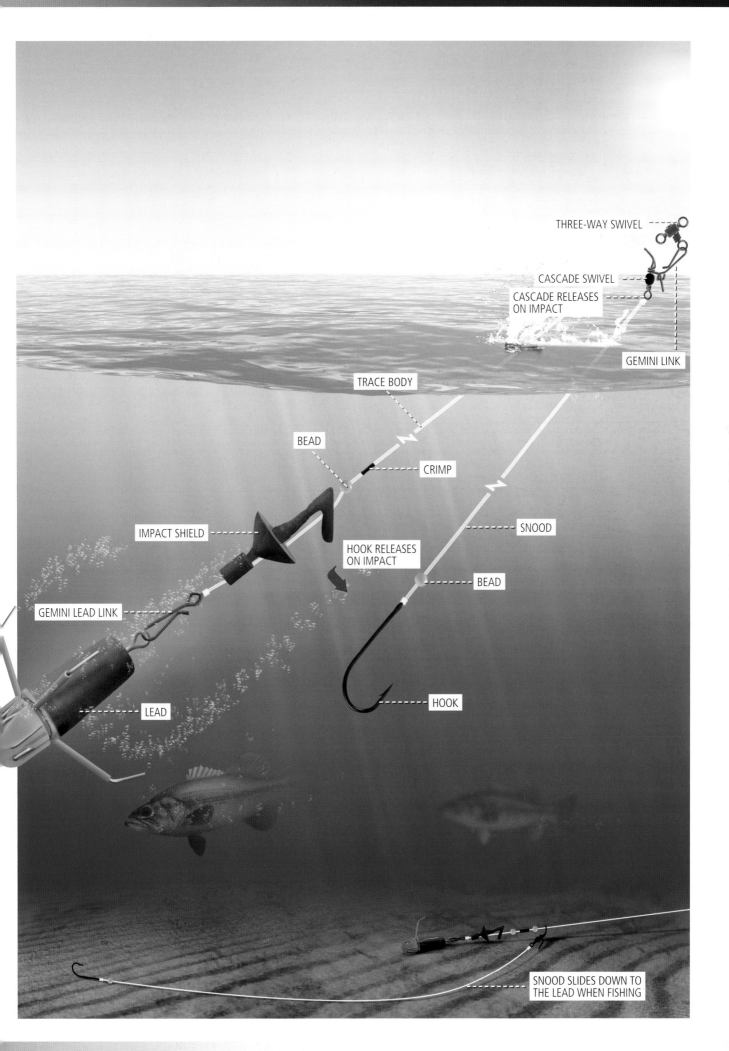

THREE-WAY SWIVEL

CASCADE SWIVEL

CASCADE RELEASES
ON IMPACT

GEMINI LINK

TRACE BODY

BEAD

CRIMP

IMPACT SHIELD

HOOK RELEASES
ON IMPACT

SNOOD

BEAD

GEMINI LEAD LINK

LEAD

HOOK

SNOOD SLIDES DOWN TO
THE LEAD WHEN FISHING

Guide To
Lures

Discover the real catching power of artificial lures.

We don't always need fresh livebait to catch fish – one of the fastest-growing aspects of sea angling is casting lures. These may be metal spinners, rigid or jointed plugs or soft-plastic lures. Self-weighted soft lures such as Red Gills and Sidewinders have proved to be very effective from the shore and afloat for bass, pollack and other predators.

Other soft lures consist of a weighted jighead with a single hook that you add a soft body to; these vary from 5g up to a hefty 385g for the Storm Wildeye Giant Shads and 460g for Savage Gear's Cutbait Herring. These have large paddle tails that wobble and

cause vibrations when trolled or retrieved and have been deadly for large cod, pollack and halibut.

The beauty of lures is that you can carry a box or bag of them plus a rod and reel in your car and you're ready to fish anytime, anywhere. You don't have delicate, smelly livebait to look after – just select a lure, clip it on and you're fishing.

It pays to carry a selection of sizes and colours of lure because fish can be fussy at times and only take a certain size or colour.

Guide To Lures

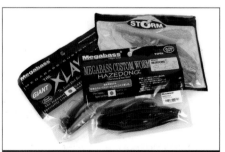

1 Metal spinners are still popular for species such as bass, mackerel and pollack.

2 Self-weighted soft plastics are very effective for many species.

3 Small jigheads can be fitted with many types of soft-plastic lures for species such as bass, pollack and wrasse.

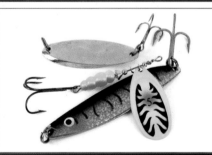

4 The heavier jigheads are best used offshore to cope with deep water and powerful tides, for fish such as cod, pollack and halibut.

5 Soft plastics are best kept in their own packets because different kinds of compounds can sometimes melt together.

6 A multi-section box is the best way to store and carry a good selection of lures.

Estuary Flounders

Flounders can be caught all round the UK coast. We tell you how to catch more of them this season.

Identification: only the flounder has a series of prickles along its forward lateral line.

Although the flounder is quite distinct looking it can often be confused with the plaice or the dab. The main distinction is that the flounder has a series of prickles along the forward lateral line, just above the pectoral fin, while the plaice has a series of raised bony knobs.

The dab has neither of these but look at the lateral line above the pectoral fin and you'll see a clear high upward curve that's unique to the dab.

Identifying a flounder as a plaice because it has faint orangey yellow spots on the top half is a common mistake made by anglers. Both of these fish can show orangey yellow spots (flounders can also occasionally crossbreed with plaice) – though typically those on the plaice are much more defined while

those on the flounder are usually diffused and lacking any real colour.

Flounders can also vary a little in colour. Over sand they can be a light fawn to dark brown, but when living on mud or shingle they can take on a grey-green coloration, sometimes with a darker mottling.

Though they're inshore fish, flounders migrate offshore into deep water to spawn, typically in the November to March period. They begin returning as thin, spent fish as early as mid-March in the south but usually mid-April further north.

Their diet is made up of worms and broken shellfish – including cockles, clams, mussels, razorfish, shrimps and crabs – but they're also somewhat predatory, often taking small fish such as sandeels and fry.

When And Where To Fish

Flounders are one of the commonest UK fish, being found right around our coast and Ireland's. They range as far north as the Faroe Islands and are even found off the southern Icelandic coast. They can also be found from the border of Russia and Norway right down the European coast and into the Mediterranean.

Juvenile flounders are resident around the UK all year but the main season for the adult fish is from mid-May to Christmas in most areas. In January and February the prolific Welsh and southwest of England estuaries are where some of the biggest flounders are caught.

The fish are found inside the smallest estuaries right through to the big main water arteries, such as the Thames and the

How To Tie A Three-Hook Boom Rig

1 Start the rig with 60 inches of clear 60lb rig-body line and tie a Gemini lead link to one end.

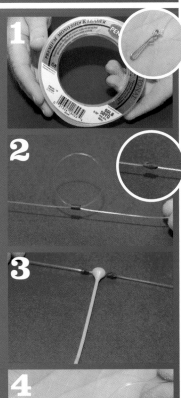

2 Slide on a short section of neoprene tubing and double the line back through this, pulling tight to form a sliding rig stop.

3 Slide on an Avis boom and form another rig stop. Add two more rig-stop and boom combinations to give you three booms on the rig body.

4 Complete the rig with a size 4 rig-connector swivel.

5 Slide the rig stops into position on the rig to space the booms apart evenly. A good combination is to place one boom at the top, one in the middle and one about 10 inches above the lead link.

6 To the booms tie on 9in to 12in, 12lb to 25lb snoods. Fluorocarbon snoods work best in all conditions, but mono is okay.

7 Sequins or beads above the hook can also give you an edge when fishing clear-water conditions. Silver and gold sequins are good choices for daylight fishing, with luminous yellow or green beads being good night-time bankers.

8 Hooks should be Kamasan B940 Aberdeens or Sakuma equivalents in sizes 2 to 6. Drop down to size 6s if bites are few and far between.

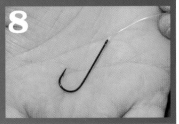

Severn estuaries. In the main estuary channel they'll be at the mouth, resident around seed mussel beds and sat inside the depressions caused by sandbanks and gutters. The deeper holes scoured out by the tide are always hotspots and flounders tend to sit in these on the inclines of the banks where the tide run is deflected. They move into side creeks and drainage channels, preferring to sit in the deeper pools where the creek forms a corner, typically sitting on the inside where the tide flow is minimal. They also travel into narrow side creeks and, as the tide floods, will move out onto shallow salt-marsh ground to feed over mud.

Flounders can often be seen sunning themselves in a few inches of water, right at the top of the tide line when living in estuary creeks. They also favour shallow harbours, living in scoured-out holes and on mud and shingle beds.

Being tolerant of freshwater, flounders will travel many miles inland up into main rivers, sometimes as much as 40 or 50 miles away from the sea where they're occasionally caught by coarse fishermen.

Flounder Tackle

In estuaries where tide flow is minimal, a spinning rod – casting 1oz to 3oz – or a mullet rod is perfect. Match this to a 4000-sized fixed-spool reel, such as the Penn Sargus or Shimano Exage, and load with 15lb to 20lb braid, adding a clear 20lb

Tip

With sliding booms you can adjust the position of the hooks. For instance, if all the fish are coming to the bottom hook when fishing deeper water, slide the bottom hook down tight behind the lead, then bring the middle hook and top hook down towards the lower boom to get all the baits fishing inside the feeding zone.

It can work in the opposite way, too, with fish only coming to the top hook so, again, adjust the lower hooks accordingly.

Flounders offer excellent sport on light tackle.

fluorocarbon leader of about 15 feet. Leads need be no more than 2oz and use Breakaways or plain bombs depending on the tide run. This tackle is more than adequate because the fish are often right at your feet; you'll rarely need to cast more than 50 yards.

In faster tides and deeper water, or when distance casting is needed, go for a bass rod, the same 4000-sized fixed-spool or a small casting multiplier such as the ABU 5500C series, and 15lb mono line with a 30lb shockleader. You may need to use 3oz to 4oz grip leads in these conditions.

Flounder Baits

Flounder baits go by season. In the March to September period, peeler or soft crab is always the most reliable, though flounders will take lug, rag and maddies (harbour rag) to a lesser degree.

When the autumn gales start and the flounders move down into the main estuary creek, crab is still good, as are worm baits, but they'll also feed on razorfish, clams and mussels. Never ignore mackerel strip as bait because they take it eagerly later on in the year, especially either side of Christmas. Try tipping a mackerel strip with maddies – it's deadly! Estuary flounders also like a section of peeler crab tipped with mackerel.

Crab.
Razorfish.
Harbour rag.

5 TopTips For Flounders

1 When baiting up with crab and fishing in very clear shallow water, add two or three peeled legs to the hook point. This gives a natural-looking presentation and encourages flounders to eat the bait from the hook point upwards, resulting in more hooked fish.

2 As you renew baits, throw the used bait into the edge of the tide and let it wash about. The smell will draw nearby flounders into the water right under your feet. You can use a swimfeeder or lead-weight feeder loaded with old bait, oils, halibut pellets and the like.

3 When using smaller baits, such as maddies, and shore crabs are stripping the bait too quickly for the flounders to find it, add a couple of float beads above the hook to lift the bait up off the sea bed a little. Flounders will see the bait and rise up off the sea bed to intercept it.

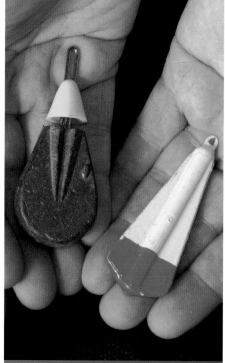

4 Flounders are attracted to movement. Always choose a lead weight light enough to roll with the tide, covering as much ground as possible and searching out the deeper holes and gutters where the flounders will sit. Or use a flat lead and twitch the bait back every now and then.

5 When working alongside creeks, the flounders will often be right on the edge of the tide line. In this situation, freelining baits such as crab and mussels, which have the weight to be cast to short range, can be deadly.

Which Beach Rod?

There are masses of beach fishing rods available on the market – but which one is best for you?

When choosing a beach fishing rod, a lot depends on where you fish and what your target species is. The rod you use when fishing clean ground for flatties and whiting, for instance, will not have enough backbone for hauling fish out of kelp and rocks.

Anglers who regularly fish rough ground and kelp prefer a stiff, powerful rod; this can be used over clean ground but would then be overgunned for the smaller species.

Rod length is another factor – most beachcasters start at 12 feet and a few are up to 18 feet long, but generally most anglers use rods between 12 and 14 feet. These give you good leverage during a cast, will keep your line above breaking waves and are designed to cast weights of 4oz to 8oz.

You should also choose a rod that most suits the distance you need or wish to achieve.

Continental-style 15ft and 16ft three-piece rods are becoming more popular nowadays. These are most often used with fixed-spool reels and allow the average angler to achieve better distances due to the extra length of the rod.

They're also used by some of the top match anglers when they need to use rigs that are 10 to 12 feet long, so the top bait can be kept in mid-water.

Bass and flattie rods could also come into this section. They're much lighter than standard beachcasters, tend to be 11 to 13 feet long and rated to cast

Shore rods need to cover many methods and species, from short-range bass and flattie bashing to hitting the horizon for cod and rays.

lighter 1oz to 4oz leads. These are ideal for close-range fishing along the shore and in estuaries where bass and flatfish feed close to the water's edge.

Another good tip – if you do a lot of night fishing, add some reflective tape to the tip because it will aid bite detection.

Choosing Your Rod

1 Continental-style 15ft and 16ft three-piece rods make distance casting easier.

2 Some are specially designed for fishing over rough ground…

3 … while others are designed for match fishing, featuring push-in fibreglass tips for the ultimate bite detection.

4 Rods designed for fixed-spool reels usually have fewer but larger rings to cut down on friction.

5 Many shore rods are fitted with sliding reel seats or coasters; this allows you to position the reel exactly where you want it.

Dig Your Own
King Rag

It's not only easy to do but it saves you money too!

This month we go digging for king rag, which are found in estuaries and rivers right across the country and often several miles from the sea on tidal mudflats. Ragworms are found in anything from soft, sloppy mud and clay to a firm, gravel/mud mixture.

Once you've found a patch of ground where rag live (look for masses of small, round holes in the mud), walk over it slowly and you'll see water squirt from the holes that the rag have made. You can start your dig with a single trench and, once you've dug for two to three feet and found a few worms, turn around and dig another trench alongside the one you've just dug. Continue this until you've covered a small patch; if you're not finding ragworms, then move on.

Once you've got the hang of it, it should be possible to dig 2lb to 3lb of fresh, lively rag in an hour. Put some scrunched-up newspaper in your bucket before you start digging, because this absorbs water and mud and makes it easier to sort out your worms when you've finished.

When you've dug enough bait, remove all the soggy paper and mud from the bucket and tip the worms onto clean, dry newspaper and sprinkle with vermiculite (you can get this from garden centres). This keeps the worms dry, toughens them and makes them easier to pick up and handle.

If you've dug a lot of worms, say around 3lb, it's best to split them up into packages of 1lb each. Wrapped in newspaper and stored in a fridge, they should keep for at least a week.

TopTips

1 Choose a fork with wide tines as this will lift soft mud and sand easier than a normal garden fork.

2 Put a few sheets of scrunched-up newspaper in your bucket to absorb water and mud.

Digging Your Own...

1 Ragworms are found on mudflats and the best digging is often found by the water's edge at low tide.

2 Digging rag is a messy job but the result is some juicy, fresh bait.

3 As you gather the worms, keep turning them over so you get fresh, dry paper at the top.

4 When you've finished digging, remove all the soggy paper and mud.

5 You should be left with a bucketful of lively rag.

6 Tip the worms onto sheets of newspaper and sprinkle with vermiculite.

The Half Blood Knot

Learn how to tie the reliable half blood knot with this essential step-by-step guide.

With a multitude of knots used for angling, choosing which one to use and then knowing how to tie it can be a nightmare.

Simple, multi-purpose knots make life so much easier and one example is the tried-and-tested half blood

knot, which has several uses including attaching line to a hook, swivel or link.

The half blood is probably the first fishing knot most of us learn to tie. It is best used with monofilament lines because braid tends to be slippery and needs more complicated, multi-turn knots.

TopTips

1 The half blood is excellent for tying hooks at night because it's so easy to do. With practice it can be done with your eyes closed.

2 Leave a 1cm tag to allow for any slippage.

3 Thin lines, such as 10lb breaking strain, need six to eight turns in the loop but three or four turns is ample for 50lb lines.

4 For extra strength you can pass the line through the hook eye twice before making the knot.

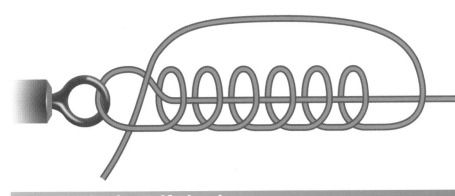

How To Tie The Half Blood

1 Pass the tag end through the hook eye.

2 Make four to eight twists, depending on line diameter.

3 Pass the tag end through the loop formed above the hook eye.

4 Lubricate the line with saliva.

5 Pull the running line smoothly and the coils will bunch up tightly.

6 Trim so that there's one centimetre of tag left and it's job done!

Three-Hook Flapper RIG

1 Start with 54 inches of 60lb mono.

2 Tie on a Gemini Lead Link at one end using a five-turn grinner knot.

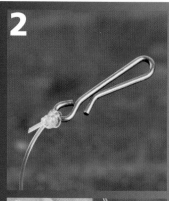

3 Slide on a rig crimp, a 3mm rig bead, a size 10 rolling rig swivel, another rig bead and a crimp. Repeat this sequence so you have three full sets of crimps, beads and swivels. Leave these loose for now.

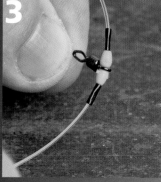

4 Complete the rig with a strong size 4 rig-connector rolling swivel, again using a five-turn grinner knot.

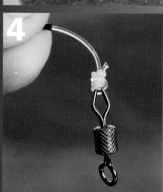

5 The first hook-trace swivel needs to be placed one inch below the rig-connector swivel. The middle swivel should be exactly 17 inches below and the third a full 32 inches below.

6 The top hook trace needs to be the longest at 15 inches; the second hook trace measures 13 inches and the bottom hook trace is the shortest at just 10 inches.

7 A 20lb hooklength is ideal when targeting smaller fish like flounders, dabs, whiting, pout and rockling, and when matched with smaller hooks like a size 2 or 1 Kamasan B940 Aberdeen. In clear seas and surf conditions switch to fluorocarbon to reduce tangles. You can also add a rubber rig-stop and sequin above the hook if you need to hold delicate ragworm and blow-lug baits neatly for perfect presentation.

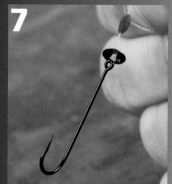

History Of The Rig

The three-hook flapper has been the mainstay of both the match and freelance angler for the past 30 years and, until recently, has seen little in the way of change with regard to its overall design.

It's based on what's commonly called a paternoster rig, meaning a series of hooks. Paternoster in this sense, as far as we can gather, has no direct reference to the Lord's Prayer (pater noster is Latin for Our Father), as some angling books have stated in the past.

Although books written in the 1900s and earlier refer to three hooks, the actual three-hook rig with the hooks positioned in sequence on the rig body only became popular during the early 1970s, and rapidly became the number-one rig during the 1980s.

The version described is designed to incorporate various hooklengths to improve presentation.

How It Works

The reason this three-hook flapper is so effective is that it positions three baits relatively close together, concentrating smell into a wider scent trail. It also allows you to experiment with different bait types fished individually. But more importantly, with combination baits on the same trace you can discover the fish's preferences on the day. This simple trick is often the key to avoiding blanks.

The most common mistake with a three-hook flapper rig is that anglers tend to make the rig with all three hook traces the same length. The problem with this is that when fishing to a tight line at close-to-medium range, the rig doesn't sit fully on the sea bed, and as each wave table passes overhead, the rig will lift in the water and bounce the baits around. At best the baits are lifting up and down above the sea bed, making a poor target for bottom fish. At worse, the upper hook bait is well above the sea bed and not fishing properly in a

fast tide run. It's no surprise then that if you ask any angler used to fishing a three-hook flapper, he'll tell you that the bottom hook closest to the lead catches the bulk of the fish.

That's why this design incorporates the longer trace at the top and the shortest hook trace at the bottom. The extra length in the upper hook trace helps keep the bait on the bottom and in the main fish-feeding zone.

When fishing at very short range in a light tide run and calmish sea, plus when fishing to a tight line, the longer middle and top hooklengths can be fished up off the sea bed. This induces a more natural movement to bait, attracting other fish that swim just off the bottom, such as whiting and coalfish.

The rig fishes well tight to a grip lead when you're deliberately fishing close to natural features such as gutters, inclines of sandbanks and hard features such as rocks and weed beds. It also fishes well when used in

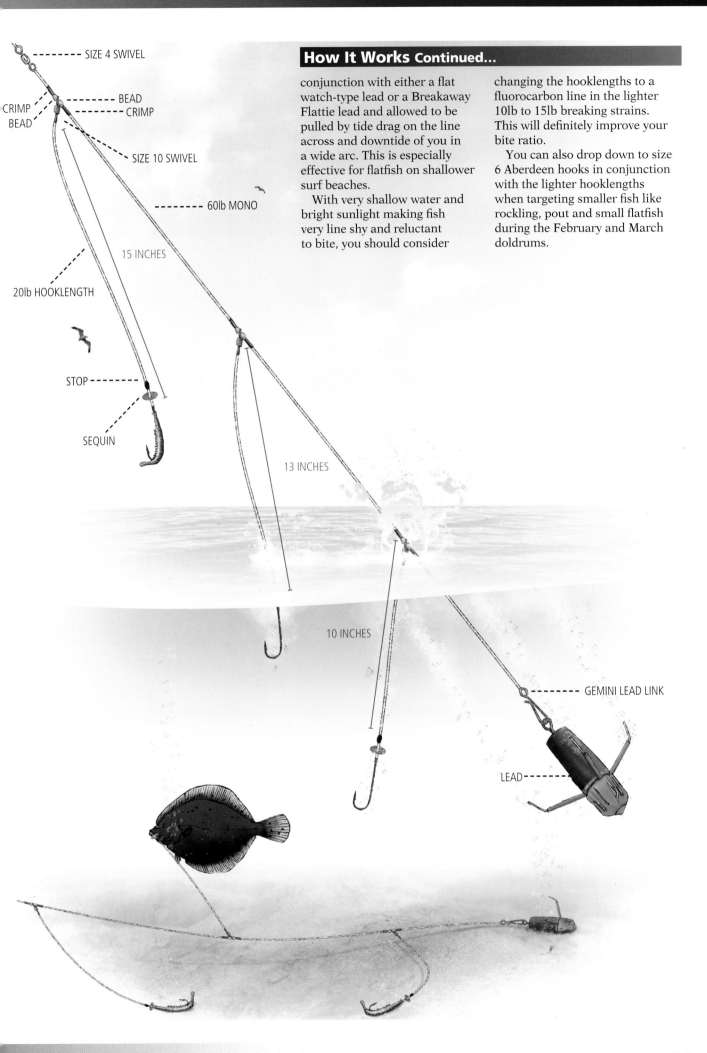

SIZE 4 SWIVEL

BEAD

CRIMP

CRIMP
BEAD

SIZE 10 SWIVEL

60lb MONO

15 INCHES

20lb HOOKLENGTH

STOP

SEQUIN

13 INCHES

10 INCHES

GEMINI LEAD LINK

LEAD

How It Works Continued...

conjunction with either a flat watch-type lead or a Breakaway Flattie lead and allowed to be pulled by tide drag on the line across and downtide of you in a wide arc. This is especially effective for flatfish on shallower surf beaches.

With very shallow water and bright sunlight making fish very line shy and reluctant to bite, you should consider changing the hooklengths to a fluorocarbon line in the lighter 10lb to 15lb breaking strains. This will definitely improve your bite ratio.

You can also drop down to size 6 Aberdeen hooks in conjunction with the lighter hooklengths when targeting smaller fish like rockling, pout and small flatfish during the February and March doldrums.

Cast The Wright Way

Barney Wright takes you through the off-the-ground cast to help you send a bait further than ever!

The off-the-ground cast (OTG) underpins all forward-facing power casts, which does include the back cast. To learn this cast is straightforward, to master it takes practice, and when you know what you're doing you'll be able to perform most other casts with ease.

The whole key to the OTG is body rotation and being smooth. The idea is to get the lead to travel as far away from the rod tip as possible and on one plane, which, in turn, will deliver lead speed and more distance with much less effort than you may expect. After all, it's the body movement and rotation that generates the power, not the body speed.

When performed well, this cast will send traces well over 150 yards with very little effort. It also helps protect the bait and, most importantly, is safe. Much less stress is put on tackle and lines than with a forced overhead cast.

Setting Up

To perform a long-range OTG-style cast, this is the basic setup. With the target being at 12 o'clock, set up your rod at eight o'clock. The line will be running off the rod tip at 135 degrees and kept tight to the lead. Your feet are at 45 degrees to the target line; in other words, right foot at 4:30 and the left at 10:30.

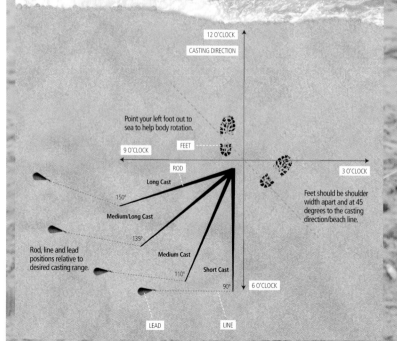

12 O'CLOCK
CASTING DIRECTION

Point your left foot out to sea to help body rotation.

FEET

9 O'CLOCK

ROD

Long Cast

150°

Medium/Long Cast

135°

Rod, line and lead positions relative to desired casting range.

Medium Cast

110°

Short Cast

90°

3 O'CLOCK

Feet should be shoulder width apart and at 45 degrees to the casting direction/beach line.

6 O'CLOCK

LEAD

LINE

01 With your right arm out to about chin height and at 90 degrees to your chest, twist your shoulders around so that the rod is at the eight o'clock position, while keeping your feet on the ground and legs slightly bent. Your right arm should be comfortably bent. Then, lean back so that nearly all of your weight is on your right foot. You should now feel twisted up like a spring.

02 Very slowly begin to undo the twist so that the rod is moving and the lead following. Your weight should begin to move forwards but still be mostly on your right side.

03 Still moving slowly, your body is untwisting; your left arm remains out and your right arm still comfortably bent but your head is beginning to turn seawards and your weight is moving forwards.

04 Now progressively increase your rotation speed while still undoing the twist, keeping your arms out. Your left hand has come up above your head and your right is in a position so that the rod tip is still low. You should have about 60 per cent of your weight on your left foot now. Begin to push off with your right foot. Note that your right arm should have adopted almost a javelin-throwing position.

05 Progressively building up lead speed, shift your weight forwards and push harder from your right foot. Look out to sea and to where you want the lead to go. You will be still undoing the twist and rotating your body. Note the left-arm position; it should also be at 90 degrees to your body and still rising. Your right arm should be comfortably bent.

06 Now power up; the lead should be beginning its upward flight path and nearly all of your weight should be on your left foot while you're still pushing with your right. The rod is now showing a bend.

07 Your cast is coming to an end and the lead should be travelling well outside the rod tip and really motoring! Turn the rod over with your left arm, using your right as a fulcrum point. If you haven't rushed the cast then you should be perfectly balanced.

08 All that's left to do now is to stop your spool as the lead hits the sea.

Events & Conferences in East Yorkshire presents

eobc

europeanopenbeachchampionship

The annual EOBC in Bridlington, East Yorkshire is the biggest three-day beach fishing festival in Europe. It attracts shore angling stars from all over the UK and Europe and offers a prize fund of up to £25,000!

Supported by:

EAST RIDING
OF YORKSHIRE COUNCIL

in association with

Total Sea FISHING

For news on this year's event and to register for tickets visit:

www.eyevents.co.uk

Contact: Paul Roggeman

T: 01482 391668   F: 01482 391679   E: info@eyevents.co.uk

Smoothhounds

When **smoothhounds** begin to show, prepare yourself for some serious summer sport with our definitive guide on how to catch them.

Smoothhounds offer fabulous summer fishing!

There are two types of smoothhound – the common and the starry – and the main difference between them is that the starry, somewhat obviously, normally has star-like spots, whereas the common has none. However, the spots can sometimes be missing from the starry so this can't be relied upon as absolute identification.

Another way to tell them apart is by the nasal flaps, which on the common are broad, and the dermal denticles, or rasping pads, on the skin, which are narrow with basal ridges but smooth ends. The starry has narrower nasal flaps and broader dermal denticles. General coloration of both species is a grey back shading to a grey/white belly.

Hounds can only really be confused with tope. The key difference is that hounds have flat, broad, grinding teeth, but the tope's teeth are triangular and sharply pointed. The tope's lower tail lobe is also long, whereas the hound's is short and blunt.

Both types of smoothhound are shallow-water fish, usually found close inshore and along the surf line, but can be found down to about 70 metres. They feed on shore crabs, hermit crabs and edible crabs, and also squat lobsters and sea anemones, but will take worms like lug and rag.

Another key factor separating the two types of smoothhound is that the common is viviparous, meaning the young are nourished from a pseudoplacenta formed by the yolk-sac membrane connected to the mother. They give birth to up to 15 young, which can measure up to 12 inches in length. The starry is ovoviviparous, with the young developed within the mother by a yolk sac, but with no membrane connection to the mother. They give birth to between seven and 15 babies, depending on the mother's size.

The breeding season is somewhat unknown, but appears to be between January and April.

The common hound is actually

How To Build An Uptiding Smoothhound Rig

1 Begin with about 24 inches of clear 60lb mono for the rig-body line.

2 Tie on a Gemini lead link at the base.

3 Slide on a rig crimp, rig bead, rig swivel, another rig bead and another rig crimp. Position the swivel about two inches above the lead link and crimp it in place.

4 Finish the main rig with a size 4 rolling rig swivel to connect to the end of the shockleader.

5 The hook trace needs to be three to six feet of 30lb/40lb mono or fluorocarbon to combat the grinding teeth of the hound. Go short in a slow-to-medium tide run, but longer in a fast tide.

6 The best hook pattern is a Mustad Viking 79515, between 2/0 and 4/0 depending on the bait size. One hook is enough as they have big mouths and, being shoaling or group fish, tend to be greedy.

less common in the UK than the starry hound. Also, the two distinct types will often be found swimming and feeding together.

When And Where

Both species can be found all around the UK coast, although the common is more southerly based and tends to venture only as far north as southern Scotland. The starry has been recorded as far north as southern Norway. To the south both species can be found as far down as the Mediterranean and off the North African coast.

Noted areas in the UK for top hound fishing are the East Coast as high as the Wash, the Thames Estuary, the Hampshire coast, both sides of the Bristol Channel, Anglesey's northwest corner and Luce Bay in Scotland.

They can be found over sandbanks and sandy gutters, and in mixed rough ground scattered among sand. They especially favour eelgrass beds, also shingle banks and any areas where big boulders break up – generally, over even, contoured ground.

Hounds are mostly caught during the day and have a habit of being over grounds for just a few tides, then disappearing. What happens is that they hunt in packs and can clean out the

food supply in a given area over two or three tides.

Rising tides from the middle-sized to the highest spring tides will invariably produce the best fishing. They like some tide run and the key time can often be the middle two hours when the run is strongest, although just after low water on some marks can be equally good.

Tackle

Uptiding rods are popular in the Wash area, the Thames Estuary and inside the Bristol Channel. But rods of 9ft 6in to 10ft and rated from 2oz to 6oz are ideal and you can match them to reels such as the ABU 6500, Penn 525 or Daiwa 7HT loaded with 15lb line and a 40lb shockleader. Only on the biggest tides when very heavy leads are needed to hold would the heavier 6oz to 10oz-rated uptiders be used, as these will overgun even the biggest of smoothhounds.

In other areas where the tide run is less harsh, most experienced anglers will opt for an 8lb to 15lb-class rod about 8ft to 8ft 6in and, again, matched to the smaller 6500 or 525-sized reels. Alternatively, load a 050/060-sized fixed-spool with 20lb braid and a 30lb shockleader when fishing lighter leads up to 4oz for maximum sport.

How To Bait Up With Crab

1 Peel all the brittle shell and legs from a peeler crab, which needs to be about the size of a 50p piece or bigger.

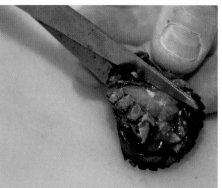

2 Cut the crab body in half lengthways.

3 Slide one half of the body up the hook and just over the hook's eye.

4 Slide the second half of the body onto the hook and leave it sitting in the bend of the hook with the hook point well exposed.

5 Bind the crab to the hook shank with a few turns of bait elastic.

Baits

A whole squid is a good bait, but make sure that the hook point is positioned in the head, otherwise they can nip off the squid's head and miss the hook.

Razorfish is good after a rough sea when there is colour in the water. Rag and squid or rag and crab cocktails also work well. Hounds will occasionally take fish baits, but these are less reliable than crab, squid and rag.

5 TopTips
For Smoothhounds

1 To reduce the effect of tide drag on the line, many anglers now use braided main line, which is much thinner in diameter for the same breaking strain than mono. Use a mono shockleader twice the length of the rod for casting and to also act as a shock absorber for fighting fish.

2 When fishing sandbanks in a light to medium tide off the stern of a boat, cast a plain lead well out, slightly uptide and beyond the other anglers. The lead will settle on the edge of a sandbank where the food is.

3 When uptide casting, don't just keep casting to the same distance and same spot – use what arc you have to explore the ground yard by yard. This can identify tiny little areas of rough ground or depressions where food will hold.

4 Smoothhound bites usually show as a series of slight knocks, followed by slack line as the fish takes the bait and turns back with the tide run, pulling the lead weight free. Wind in the slack line until the weight of the fish is felt then set the hook with an upward strike.

5 Hounds have tough mouths, so make sure to use a hook sharpener on non-chemically sharpened hook points to make sure they are ultra-sharp. A knife-edge pattern such as the Mustad Viking 79515 can be honed to an ultra-sharp cutting edge and is a popular choice. Alternatively, look at the Sakuma 540 Manta Extra, which is strong and chemically sharpened with a wide gape.

How To Use
Blueys

Blueys are full of oils and scent, making it an ideal bait for any species. Here's how to use it.

Blueys are actually Pacific saury, and get their nickname from their blue colour. They're very oily fish, like mackerel, but with far more oil and blood that creates a greater scent trail and attracts more fish. On the minus side, they have very soft flesh and need to be bound securely to the hook with fine elastic. They're a bit too big to be used whole but can be cut in half to make two big baits for congers, cod and bass – they've tempted several double-figure bass already.

Other ways to use them are to cut them into chunks for rays and bass or take a fillet off one side and use part of this for bait.

For a more streamlined bait, cut your fillet down the middle to give a long, thin strip. Cut the strip in half so that it's about six or seven inches long, put the hook through the middle of the strip then double it back up the snood and bind it on with elastic. This makes a sausage-shaped bait, oozing oil and blood, that can be cast a long way and is very effective for rays, doggies, bass or congers.

Blueys are frozen in packs of two or three, so you can keep a supply in your freezer and take what you need for a session in a cool box. You can thaw one out as you need it and keep the others frozen.

You can get several baits from a single fillet.

Streamlined Bait

1 To make a streamlined bait, cut the fillet down the middle with a pair of scissors.

2 Put the hook through the middle of the strip…

3 … then double it back over the hook and up the snood.

4 Secure the fillet in place with fine elastic.

Joining Two
Running Lines

Learn how to tie two running lines together with the uni-to-uni knot.

It is important to change your lines every few sessions as they will get damaged. It isn't always necessary to strip all the line off, though – simply remove the amount of line you use plus 50 yards or so. For example, if you can cast 100 yards, then 150 yards is ample. Just strip off the line as far back into the spool as necessary. Now join the new line to the spool line.

Although this knot is unlikely to ever leave the spool, it might do if you're playing a big fish or if there's a big bow in a fast tide. So, for this reason, use a knot that keeps the line as strong as possible.

TopTips

1 Always use saliva to lubricate as you tie knots.

2 Four or five turns in the uni knot are ample; too many and it can make the knot weaker.

3 Never pull the knots tight before pulling them together – pull them taut, then tighten as the knots meet.

How To Tie The Uni-To-Uni Knot

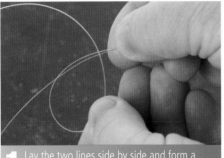
1 Lay the two lines side by side and form a loop with one tag end.

2 Pass the tag end through the loop four times, then lubricate and pull taut.

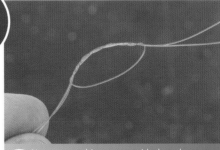
3 Now repeat this process with the other tag end.

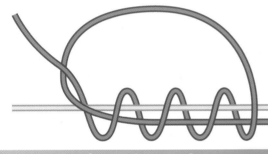
4 Lubricate and slowly draw the two knots together…

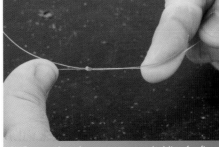
5 … and apply even pressure, holding for five seconds. Do not tug at the knot because this will weaken the line.

6 Trim the tag ends and you're done.

The Pulley RIG

History Of The Rig

The pulley rig seems to have originated in both South Wales and the northeast of England around 20 years ago.

The initial pulley-principle idea was taken from the standard sliding-leger rig but changed to fish as a normal fixed paternoster rig would. The pulley idea was thought up as anglers in the two named areas were fishing rough ground on a day-to-day basis. They were losing gear and fish when using traditional paternoster rigs due to the trailing lead snagging in the rough ground as the rig or fish was being retrieved.

Although initially designed for rough ground, it also became popular with anglers fishing the shore for rays and tope over clean ground, albeit in a much-modified form.

How It Works

The main advantage of the pulley rig is that when a fish takes the bait, it has the power to pull the hooklength and rig body through the pulley-rig bead and physically lift the lead up out of the snags.

Once the rig body is pulled through the swivel, until it hits the bead above the Impact Shield, the lead is up in the water and above the snags.

The pulley rig works best when casting into a good depth of water. When fishing at range in shallow water, the rig lays too flat on the sea bed, and as a fish takes the bait and pulls against the lead, this action can drag a lead deep into a snag.

In deep water, due to the raised angle of the line, the lead tends to literally lift upwards and out of a snag. Pulley rigs are not a good choice for very shallow-water fishing!

Due to the pulley principle, the rig also acts as a self-striking rig. As the fish takes the bait it can pull only minimum line before it comes up tight against the full weight of the rising and sliding lead. It's the weight of the lead that creates the self-striking effect.

Another attribute of the pulley rig is that it can be made to a longer length than other rigs, but remains only half its total length for casting. This means that when the lead reaches the stop bead you have a full length of heavy mono that resists abrasion from fish with rough skin, rocks and barnacles when retrieving big fish over rough ground.

Most anglers choose to build this rig incorrectly by replacing the more expensive pulley-rig bead with a standard-eyed swivel, but powerful casters have found that when using a standard swivel, the thin-diameter wire of the eye concentrates pressure on the same tiny section of rig body with every cast. This weakens this section of the line and, inevitably, it will part. This occurs during the main power of the cast, resulting in rig-body breakage and the lead weight flying down the beach and causing a potential injury, or fatality, to anybody in the firing line.

The rig described with the Impact Shield is designed when maximum-range casting is required. To save on rig

Build Sequence

1 Start with 50 inches of 80lb rig-body line.

2 To one end of the rig body, tie on a Gemini lead link.

3 Slide on a Breakaway Impact Shield followed by a 3mm bead and crimp. Leave around one-and-a-half millimetres for the Impact Shield to slide, to avoid hook-snood stretch during the cast.

4 Above the crimp, slide on a 5mm bead, a Fox pulley-rig bead and another 5mm bead.

5 Measure the free end of line, leaving it slightly shorter than the main rig body, and tie a double figure-of-eight knot in it to form the hooklength.

6 Tie on either a single size 4/0 Viking pattern hook for rays or, alternatively, us a 3/0 or 4/0 two-hook Pennel rig. When using a single hook, tie in, above the hook, a Powergum sliding stop knot to act as a bait stop when casting.

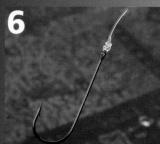

How It Works Continued...

components when tackle losses will be heavy and distance is less important, do away with the Impact Shield assembly altogether and replace the Gemini lead link with a Gemini bait clip. The hook then just sits in the bait clip, but this rig will not fly as far due to the increased air friction of the bait and not being streamlined by the shield.

When fishing mixed rough ground with heavier 30lb reel line and using a weak-link system to the lead weight, you can also reduce losses by putting a swivel where the figure-of-eight knot should go on the rig body, then adding a hook snood slightly lighter than your main reel line. This will break should the hook get snagged, but remember that a lighter hook snood may also cost you fish.

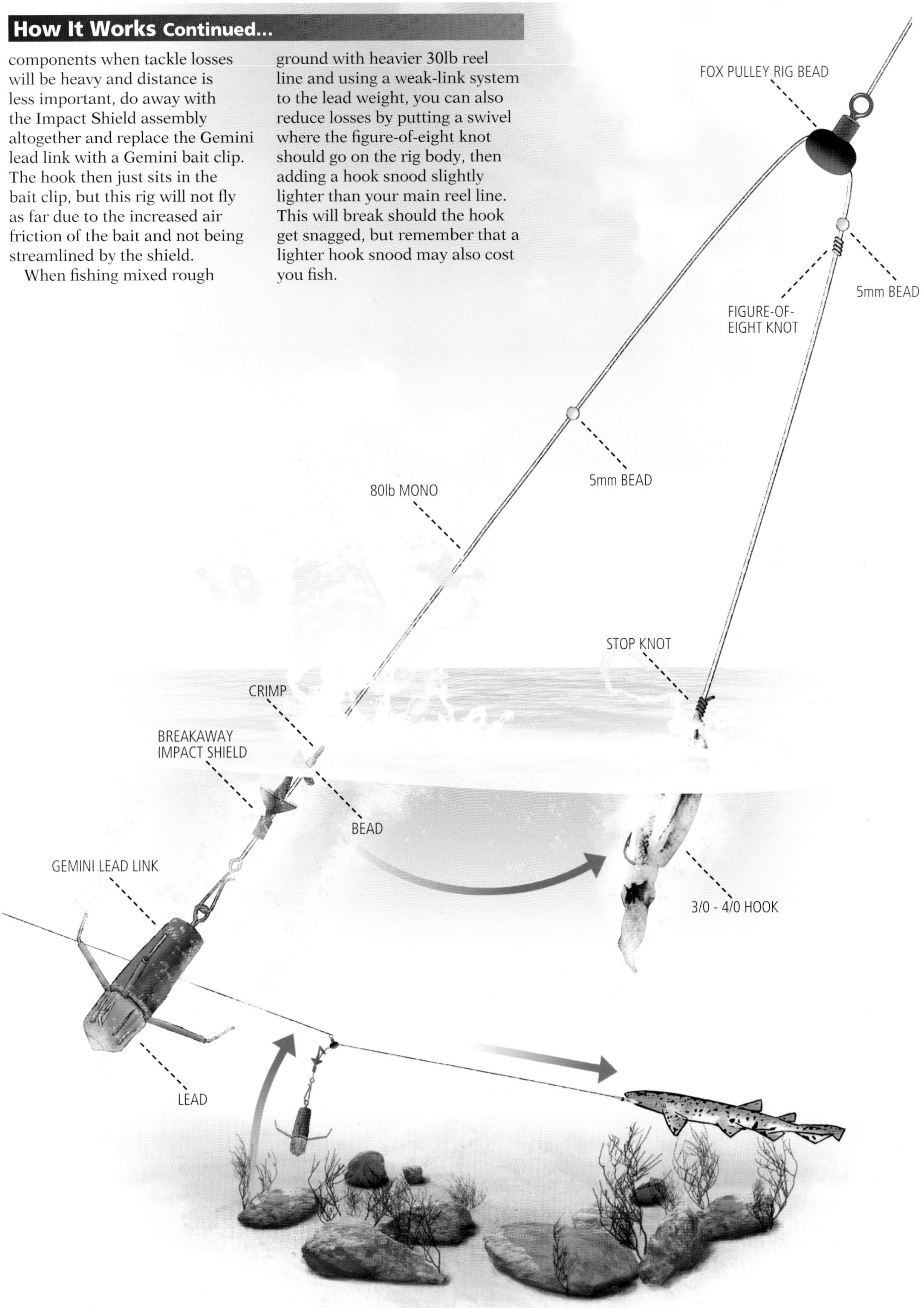

FOX PULLEY RIG BEAD

5mm BEAD

FIGURE-OF-EIGHT KNOT

5mm BEAD

80lb MONO

STOP KNOT

CRIMP

BREAKAWAY IMPACT SHIELD

BEAD

GEMINI LEAD LINK

3/0 - 4/0 HOOK

LEAD

Rough-Ground Cod

Cod are fun to catch and good to eat. We show you where, when and how to maximise your chances of catching more!

Cod remain, arguably, the UK angler's favourite sea fish, partly because of the rough and tough environment and conditions we fish for them in, but also because they put up a decent fight from the shore and also taste good on a plate.

The only fish the cod can really be confused with is its near cousin the whiting. The cod, though, has a more blunt head shape, with the whiting being more pointed. The lateral line on the cod is also more pronounced with an upward curve above the pectoral fin. The whiting also carries a definite black spot at the root of its pectoral fin, whereas the cod doesn't.

Cod range widely in colour. Over sand they are a mottled fawn or brown on the back with a white underside, but over mixed ground become a mottled green, yet when living around kelp weed beds they can be a dull reddy-orange.

Cod are eating machines and have a wide diet. They take small crustaceans and crabs, worms and brittle stars when small, but as they pack on weight they start to become more predatory, favouring small cod, whiting, herring, mackerel, sandeels, pout and poor cod. The average size nowadays for UK cod is between 1lb and 5lb, but double-figure fish are always on the cards and 20lb specimens still feature off the beaches occasionally. Cod in excess of 200lb were recorded in the 1800s by longliners over the Grand Banks, and 100lb-plus fish are still sometimes caught commercially and taken in to fish factories in Iceland and Norway. The chance of a monster still remains!

Tackle

Tackle needs to be tough to handle the conditions and to work good-sized fish back through multiple snags. Choose a stiff, 6oz, fast-taper beachcaster,

Rough-Ground Cod Pulley Rig

1 Take 60 inches or so of clear 60lb/80lb Sufix Zippy trace line or a similar brand. To one end tie on a Gemini lead link.

2 Now slide on a Breakaway Impact Shield or a bait clip, adding a bead and crimp above. Crimp the crimp in place, leaving about an inch for the Shield/bait clip to slide in.

3 Slide on a 5mm bead, a Fox pulley rig bead or a plain rolling swivel and another 5mm bead, then tie on a big swivel.

4 Leaving about 30 inches of free hook trace, form a 6in to 8in loop and tie in a double granny knot to secure the loop.

5 Onto the doubled hook trace, slide on an 8mm bead followed by a size 4/0 Mustad Viking 79510 hook. Leaving about an inch and a half for the top hook to slide freely in, tie in another granny knot.

6 On the single loop below, slide on either a 4/0 or 6/0 Viking 79515 hook by passing the end of the loop through the eye and then down over the hook and pulling tight.

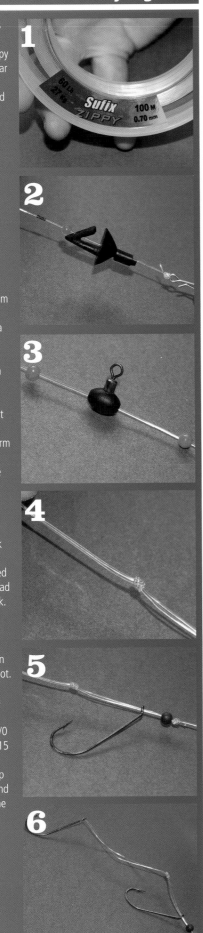

Note:

The pulley rig bead is better than a plain swivel because the thin wire of a normal swivel eye will stretch and damage mono line during repeated power casts. The pulley rig bead spreads the load over a wider area, avoiding this, plus it gives a smoother pulley effect than the plain swivel will.

This double hook gives a stronger biting trace, which is necessary due to the cod having abrasive mouths, plus it helps protect the crucial hook end from abrasion caused by rocks when dragging the fish back through rocks and kelp.

Strong reels are needed to cope with heavy ground.

ideally between 12ft 6in and 13ft 6in. For longer casting over mixed rough and mixed heavy ground, the Penn 525 is the most favoured reel by the majority of anglers due to its gear strength. Load this with 18lb to 22lb line and a 60lb to 80lb shockleader.

For really rough ground, then the ABU 7000 type multiplier or Penn 535 are popular, as well as the Daiwa Slosh 30. Load these with 25lb to 30lb line and a shockleader. This tackle allows you to really bully fish back through the kelp and snags.

When And Where To Fish

Cod can be caught over rough ground for most of the year, but the best of the fishing is from September, peaking between November and late January, with some areas experiencing a secondary spring run from late March to late April generally speaking.

Good rough-ground areas are the east coast of Scotland, the northeast of England down as far as Whitby, the South Wales coast as far west as Stout Point, and the Cumbrian coast. Parts of the west Scottish coast and the coast of Northern Ireland can also give good rock fishing at times.

The type of ground to look for is either mixed stone and boulders spaced with small patches of sand or, better still, solid rough ground with deep lateral gutters and channels. Deep fissures running shorewards with kelp growth evident is also good.

Water depth is not overly important because cod will come right in to shallow surf to feed on the flooding tide, but generally look for a consistent depth of six feet plus to provide consistent fishing.

In rough, coloured seas cod will feed by day, but in many areas the top anglers only choose to fish at night as the cod move closer to shore during the hours of darkness.

When fishing shallow-water surf beaches into mixed ground, the bigger spring tides falling the three days before and after the highest tide tend to give the best fishing. That said, over very rough ground, even neap tides can produce fish because the water is a more consistent depth and the fish stay closer to shore, providing that the sea is rough and coloured.

10 TopTips For Cod

1 When fishing into very rough ground, use a weak-link system to the lead. One of the simplest, and the best, is to make lead weights with a simple wire dog-leg of wire in the top instead of an eye. You can then tie a weak link of 15lb line to the lead link and to the wire on the lead, then put the angle of the dog-leg in the wire into the link. When the lead hits the sea bed, the wire will slide out of the link and leave the lead held only by the weak link of line.

2 During the pre-Christmas period a big lugworm bait will catch the bulk of the cod. Make your bait by pushing two or three worms on the hook, with size depending upon the hook, then putting two more worms alongside the hook bait splint-style and wrap the whole lot together with bait elastic to form a big sausage shape about six to eight inches long.

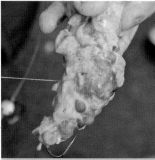

3 In the early new-year period, cod in many areas begin to lose interest in worm-based baits and will take big mussel baits, again made with multiple mussels pushed up the hook and bound on with bait elastic to form a sausage shape about four to six inches long. Mussel is especially effective along the east Scottish shore and in the northeast of England, but will catch fish anywhere.

4 Most rock marks fish best during the flooding tide, especially the rock gullies in deeper water. However, when fishing offshore reef ground, fish will often move along the beach with the flood tide, but drop back again over the same ground on the ebb, though they tend to be at longer range. This means that an ebb tide at night might well outfish the perfect flood tide by day.

5 Cod bites are typically a double thump on the rod tip, then a full pull down. Most cod hook themselves, but it's best to lift the rod, wind in the slack line until you feel the fish, then set the hook to make sure against the full weight of the fish.

6 If a fish is hooked and becomes snagged on the way in, give it a few feet of free line and lower the rod tip slightly. Often the fish will swim the lead weight free of the snag as it swims back away from you and you'll realise this as the line tightens again to the weight of the fish.

7 In the more southern areas of England after late January, cod become scarcer as they move offshore, but those left inshore late will have a preference for fresh peeler crab if you can get it.

8 If you catch one cod from a certain position in a certain gully, try to cast back to exactly the same position. Cod are predictable and fish will favour certain specific areas to feed above all others.

9 The best tip of all is to target cod when the sea is rough with a good surf running. Ideal conditions often fall just as a full gale has blown through and the sea is just beginning to lose its full swell. Cod are powerful swimmers and have no problem feeding in rough surf seas.

10 Worm baits can often be made more effective by tipping them off with mussel and queen cockles, especially after a gale has washed shellfish up onto the shore. Tipping with squid strip is also effective.

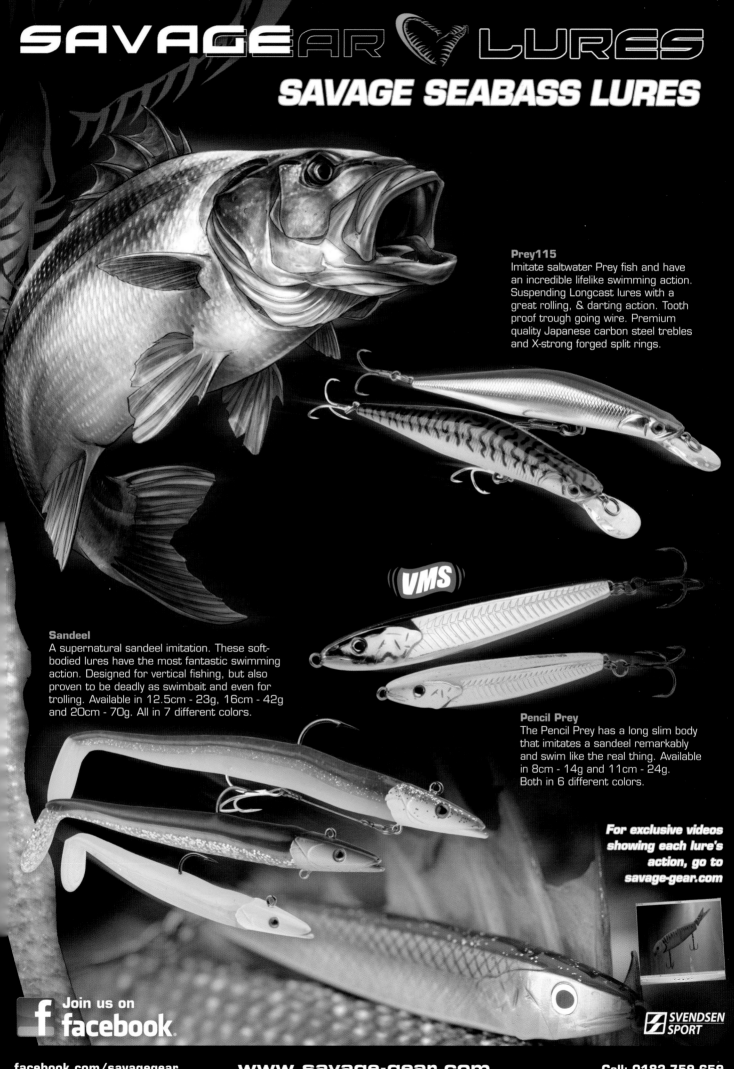

SAVAGEAR LURES

SAVAGE SEABASS LURES

Prey115
Imitate saltwater Prey fish and have an incredible lifelike swimming action. Suspending Longcast lures with a great rolling, & darting action. Tooth proof trough going wire. Premium quality Japanese carbon steel trebles and X-strong forged split rings.

Sandeel
A supernatural sandeel imitation. These soft-bodied lures have the most fantastic swimming action. Designed for vertical fishing, but also proven to be deadly as swimbait and even for trolling. Available in 12.5cm - 23g, 16cm - 42g and 20cm - 70g. All in 7 different colors.

Pencil Prey
The Pencil Prey has a long slim body that imitates a sandeel remarkably and swim like the real thing. Available in 8cm - 14g and 11cm - 24g. Both in 6 different colors.

For exclusive videos showing each lure's action, go to savage-gear.com

Join us on facebook

SVENDSEN SPORT

facebook.com/savagegear   **www.savage-gear.com**   Call: 0182 759 659

Mussels

A little bit of time and effort will see you fishing with a plentiful supply of free and highly effective bait.

Mussels are common bivalves that can be found in their millions all around the country but are often overlooked as bait. This is possibly due to the amount of work involved in collecting them and shucking them from their shells. They're found in clumps clinging to harbour walls, pier piles, rocks and many large estuaries.

They constitute a natural food for many species and – despite the time-consuming, messy preparation – they make excellent bait for cod, bass, whiting, wrasse and flatfish from both the shore and boat. The trick is to scoop a few dozen out of their shells at home and store them in a plastic box with a lid on. Then, when you're out fishing, thread several onto the hook and up the snood and bind them securely with fine bait elastic. They won't stand up to powerful casting but long casts aren't usually necessary as most mussel beds are near the shore anyway. If you're boat fishing, simply lower them over the side.

Another method is to use something like Fox Arma Mesh bait tubing. It's not PVA so it doesn't dissolve in water, and you pack your mussels into it to form a sausage, then simply put your hook through the sausage, cast out and wait for a bite. If you don't live near the sea and can't pick your own mussels, you can buy them from your local supermarket and any excess can be frozen down for a later date.

Mussels often live in huge groups so collecting a good supply is easy.

How To Bait Up With Mussels

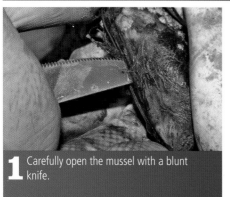
1 Carefully open the mussel with a blunt knife.

2 Once open, you can see the juicy flesh inside.

3 Carefully scoop the mussel from its shell.

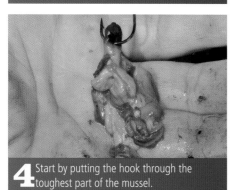
4 Start by putting the hook through the toughest part of the mussel.

5 Once you have three, four or five mussels on the hook, secure them with fine bait elastic.

6 Here's your bait, ready to go.

The Twisted Boom

Learn how to tie the twisted boom – a cheap and effective way to make bait stand away from the trace for great bait presentation.

When fishing over rough ground or kelp, or off a pier, booms are great for helping you present your bait most effectively. Using a boom will make your snood stand away from the trace body and help prevent tangles, which, in turn, makes the trace fish more efficiently.

The problem is that booms cost a bit but are great for fishing snaggy areas – so this is where twisted booms come into their own.

A twisted boom requires no extra components so, if lost, you will only lose the hooks and a few pence worth of line. They can be tied easily at the venue in a matter of minutes and they give you the confidence to cast into snaggy areas where you normally wouldn't dare!

TopTips

1 Use saliva to lubricate the knot when tightening.

2 You can trap a swivel in the boom if you wish.

3 Ensure you have at least 12 inches of each tag after forming the twisted boom.

4 You can adjust the length of the trace by cutting it from the spool to the desired length.

How To Make The Twisted Boom

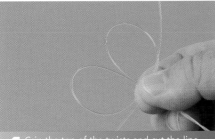

1 Pull off a 3ft section of 80lb mono and tie a 2in single overhand loop in the end.

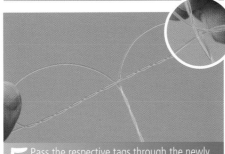

2 Place your foot on the spool and pop your index and middle fingers through the overhand loop, then rotate 30 times or so to put twists in the line.

3 Use your free hand to pinch at the centre of the line to start the twisted boom. Now release the pressure between the spool and your hand and the boom will form.

4 Grip the top of the twists and cut the line from the spool to remove the overhand loop. Pass one tag to the left over the top of the twisted boom and the other to the right and beneath it.

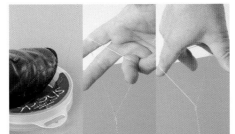

5 Pass the respective tags through the newly formed loops four or five times.

6 Lubricate, grip the end of the twisted boom in your teeth and pull it tight. Attach whatever you wish to either end, be it swivels or links, to suit whatever rig you're going to use.

The Northeast Rough-Ground Cod RIG

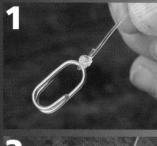

History Of The Rig

This is one of the simplest and oldest rigs – it has changed little over the past 50 years – yet it remains popular to this day. This basic rig has actually been around for 150 years or more and was first used when Cuttyhunk, a twisted linen-type line, was the main line used through the 1800s and early 1900s for angling in the UK prior to the introduction of mono.

It's often referred to as the northeast rough-ground cod rig – the reason being that the rough ground and kelp weed, found predominantly along the northeast coast of England, claims vast amounts of tackle, so anglers like this rig because it uses minimal components and costs less to lose.

The rig is used nationally, though, and not just for cod but for any situation that sees you casting into rough ground when after bass, wrasse and other rock dwellers.

How It Works

This is basically a simple paternoster rig with the stand-off loop holding the hook snood slightly out from the main rig body. Using 80lb mono for the rig body means that the rig has the strength to be cast out to reasonable distances in conjunction with a 60lb shockleader, or can be cast to close range when using 30lb to 40lb mono straight through – as some anglers prefer to do.

Also, the 80lb line will inevitably come into direct contact with the rocks, barnacles and sharp mussel shells associated with rough-ground fishing, but the diameter of this line usually means it can withstand occasional nicks and scars without weakening.

Many rough-ground anglers prefer to attach the lead direct to the bottom oval split ring and rely on the overall strength of the tackle to pull a snagged weight free. This is done by hand and never direct to the reel or rod as reel spindles can bend and rods break if put under undue stress.

Alternatively, you can replace the original bottom oval split ring with a cheap weak-link system. This can be created by attaching an inverted, Gemini clipped-down lead link. The lead is clipped onto the link for casting and will release on impact with the water. A 12in section of 10lb line is tied between the lead and the link eye for the 'weak link'.

The choice of the Mustad Viking hook pattern is also important. Although this hook is ultra-strong and proven over decades, it will straighten under severe pressure and release itself from snags, and in rough ground that can save countless rigs. Modern hooks, such as Sakuma and Varivas, as good as they are, won't straighten and will invariably snap, hence the specific Viking 79515 pattern recommendation for this rig.

An inverted Gemini clip makes a perfect weak-link system.

LINK

INVERTED GEMINI CLIPPED-DOWN LEAD LINK

LOOP

WEAK LINK

LEAD RELEASES ON IMPACT

SNOOD

LEAD

HOOK

IF THE LEAD IS SNAGGED, THE WEAK LINK WILL BREAK TO RELEASE THE RIG.

Multiplier Braking Systems

This shows the two types of braking system – centrifugal on the top and magnetic on the bottom.

We take a look at magnetic and centrifugal braking systems.

The two main types of braking systems in multiplier reels are centrifugal and magnetic. A third is mechanical, where either the left or right-hand knob is tightened against the end of the spool spindle – but this can cause damage if overdone, so we'll concentrate on how to set the centrifugal and magnetic systems.

The centrifugal braking works by tiny brake blocks rubbing against the inside of a brake drum, located inside the reel's endplate. There can be anything from one to six blocks that can be put to use.

This system helps to avoid overruns, because the faster the spool spins, the harder the blocks rub against the drum and stop it from spinning too fast.

Obviously, the more or larger brake blocks you use, the harder the braking, but it will also cut down on overall distance.

Magnets work in a different way because there is no actual contact and the braking comes from a magnetic field – the closer the magnets are to the spinning spool, the greater the braking effect; the further away the magnets are from the spool, the less the braking effect. Once again, the number, size and power of the magnets will have different braking results. Some reels are fitted with up to six magnets, whereas others only have one very powerful magnet.

All these reels, however, need to be set up correctly, so here we'll take a step-by-step look at how the magnet and brake-block systems actually work.

Guide To Braking Systems

1 The centrifugal system works when the spool spins and throws the brake blocks against the brake drum.

2 Modern reels have up to six small blocks…

3 … whereas older models may only have two large blocks.

4 Magnetic reels may have one powerful magnet – or a bank of several magnets.

5 Magnets control the spool revolutions by way of a magnetic field. Here the magnets are moved closer to the spool for full braking…

6 … and away for less braking.

THE BREAKAWAY COLLECTION 2011

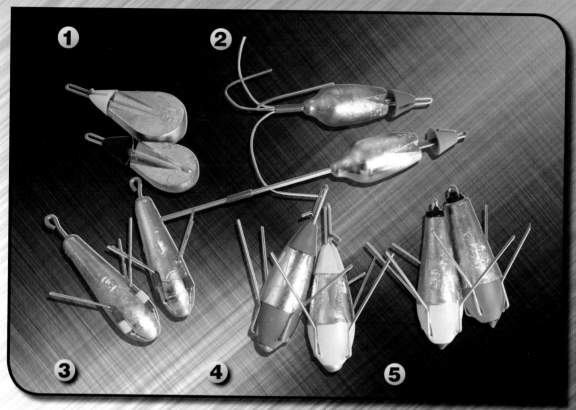

1. **Impact Flattie** - Available in 85g & 150g
2. **Impact Softy Lead** - Available in 150g, 170g & 200g
3. **Standard Breakaways** - Available in short tail & long tail, 90g to 210g
4. **Impact Leads** - Available in 125g, 150g, 170g & 200g
5. **Ultra Leads & Moulds** - Available in 150g & 170g

- Ultra Big Butt – new this year
- Better bait protection because of the contoured body
- Designed to be used with the Imp
- In-flight stability – Even with a side wind

The Breakaway range of tackle should be available from a tackle dealer near you.

Breakaway
TACKLE DEVELOPMENT CO LTD
376 Bramford Road, Ipswich IP1 5AY Telephone 01473 832822

www.breakaway-tackle.co.uk

Shore Whiting

It's that time when the **whiting** show up, so be prepared with our expert advice on how to bag up with them from the shore…

There's good sport to be had when the whiting show.

The whiting is a member of the cod family, and you can distinguish the whiting from the cod by looking at the dorsal fin. On the whiting the rear of the dorsal fin is inside the first anal fin, but on the cod the rear edge of the dorsal finishes in front of the first anal fin when the fish is viewed side on. The whiting's body is also more slender than the cod's.

The colour of the whiting is generally sandy brown when it lives over sand, but sometimes greeny blue when over shingle, with the sides and belly silvery white. The whiting also carries a black spot at the root of the pectoral fin.

The whiting is found all around the British Isles and Ireland, as well as Iceland, the outer Baltic,

off the Norwegian coast to the Russian border and also south along the northern side of the Mediterranean.

The whiting inhabits sandy and muddy bottoms down to depths of 200 metres, though usually much shallower.

The whiting's diet consists of sandeels, small herring, sprats, worms and small crustaceans – especially shrimps.

The whiting can spawn between January and July, but mainly between January and April and in shallow water close to the shore. Juvenile whiting are often to be found living among jellyfish tentacles, to whose sting they are immune.

Very few whiting make 2lb in weight and in many areas a 1lb fish off the shore is a very good

catch. The exceptions to this are the deeper beaches such as Dungeness in Kent and Chesil Beach in Dorset, where 2lb whiting are much more common. Big whiting can also show off the rocks in the west of Ireland, especially in Donegal.

When And Where To Fish

The shore-whiting season is traditionally from early September through to late January, but peaks between late October and early December from the shallower beaches. On the deeper beaches, and when fishing from breakwaters and rocks into deep water, the season can last longer and well into January, with the biggest fish appearing right at the death in mid to late January.

How To Build A Three-Hook Flapper Rig For Whiting

1 Start with 54 inches of 60lb mono.

2 Tie on a Gemini lead link at one end.

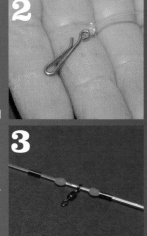

3 Slide on a crimp, a 3mm rig bead, a size 10 rolling swivel, another rig bead and a crimp. Repeat this sequence to give you three full sets. Leave these loose for now.

4 Complete the rig with a strong size 4 rig-connector rolling swivel.

5 The first hook-trace swivel needs to be crimped one inch below the rig-connector swivel. The middle swivel should be 17 inches down and the third a full 32 inches down.

6 The top hook trace needs to be the longest at 15 inches, the second should measure 13 and the bottom one be the shortest at just 10. Mono hook traces are okay, but fluoro hooklengths are slightly stiffer and tangle less when surf fishing. Use 20lb hooklengths for standard fishing, but if you're getting a succession of bigger whiting, their sharp teeth can mince through lighter mono, so a change to tougher 25lb fluoro guards against fish chewing through the line. Only fish as heavy as you need to on the hook traces because whiting like a moving bait.

7 Good hooks are Kamasan B940 Aberdeens in size 2 or the Sakuma and Mustad equivalents.

This rig is ideal for flood-tide and general fishing when the fish are at close to medium range and will maximise your catches. On the ebb, good anglers will switch to two-hook clipped-up rigs for maximum casting range, because the fish will move much further out on the ebb when working in shallow water.

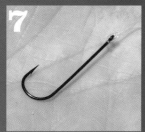

Cold, frosty nights with bright stars and no moon are rated the best for whiting and they generally like calm seas, though the bigger fish will run a surf much as bass do in the post-Christmas period. Rough weather and big seas push the whiting out to deeper water and out of range of the shore angler.

On the shallow surf beaches, darkness triggers a mass invasion of whiting inshore but, ideally, the tide needs to coincide with or fall in darkness. Daylight tides tend not to be productive. The bigger tides produce the best fishing, though in deeper water neap tides will also produce good numbers of fish.

Breakwaters and other man-made structures offering deeper water will produce some fish by day, especially if the water carries some colour, but, again, nightfall sees a dramatic increase in catches.

Whiting Tackle

Off the beaches when the whiting are close in, a 2oz to 4oz bass rod with an ABU 5000-sized reel is ideal, and gives good sport with sizeable whiting. Load the reels with 12lb mono, a 30lb

Whiting come in to feed in the shallows as the sun sets.

An ABU 5000 or 6000 reel is ideal.

shockleader and use leads of no more than 3oz.

When greater casting distance is needed and when fishing into deeper water, a 4oz to 6oz beachcaster, ABU 6500, Penn 525 or Daiwa 7HT series reel loaded with 15lb line and a 60lb shockleader is perfect.

Top Whiting Baits

Adult whiting are major predators and feed primarily on fish. Strips of mackerel, herring, bluey, sprat and even strips of their own kind will pick out the bigger fish in the shoal. Squid can also be good on its day, but is not as consistent as oily fish. The favourite big-whiting bait is a half-body from a 5in sandeel.

Lug and rag tend to target the smaller fish, with razorfish sometimes fishing okay after a storm.

If you use worm baits, then tipping the hook point with a small strip of mackerel can help you pick out the bigger whiting in the shoal. Also, when whiting are ripping at the worm but missing the hook, adding the strip of mackerel to the hook point encourages them to take the bait where the hook point is.

Watch out for the whiting's needle-like teeth.

Lugworm tipped with mackerel is great bait.

5 TopTips For Whiting

1 Always identify the deeper gullies that run along the beach, or the seaward side of sandbanks. The inclines of the gutters and banks will hold sandeels and shrimps, which are main food sources of inshore whiting. Also, any food washed along by the tide flow will fall into the gutters and the whiting will swim along these looking for food.

2 During the flood tide the whiting shoals will be tight in among the breakers, so aim to cast 30 to 40 yards to find the fish. But, as the tide peaks and begins to ebb, they will move out to long range and casts in excess of 125 yards may be required to remain in contact with fish.

3 When fishing into deep water, say off a breakwater, a three-hook flapper is less effective because it will be fishing vertically and not at a shallow angle with all the baits on the sea bed as it should be. In this situation use a rig with a long flowing hook trace positioned tight behind the lead weight. Add a second hook using a three-turn water knot halfway along – this will keep the baits on the sea bed where the whiting expect to find them and you'll catch more fish.

4 When the tide is flowing strongly, whiting will usually hook themselves on shorter hook snoods of nine inches. But as the tide eases you'll see the bites and often miss the fish – when this occurs, lengthen the snoods up to 15 to 18 inches. This extra length gives the whiting the freedom of movement to pick up the bait, turn with the tide and build up some swimming speed to help set the hook.

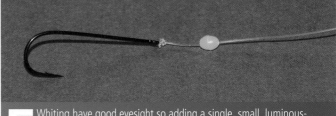

5 Whiting have good eyesight so adding a single, small, luminous-green bead above the hook at night can increase the catch rate. Whiting are drawn to the luminescence, which in the autumnal surf is a natural occurrence due to phosphorescent plankton.

How To Use
Mackerel

Catch, prepare and store this juicy bait for the hook.

Mackerel are easy to find. You can catch your own, buy them fresh from a fishmonger or supermarket, or get them blast frozen from your local tackle shop.

When the mackerel are 'in' during the summer months, it's easy to bag up with dozens of them, so only take what you need for food or bait.

You will catch your share of mackerel on feathers, spinners and floats, and while casting feathers will catch you more, spinning and float fishing with light tackle is more fun.

Being a common, natural food, mackerel can be fished as bait in just about every sea – whether you're using the whole fish or just a tiny strip. A strip of mackerel can be used on its own or to tip off other baits to add flavour and colour for bottom rigs and float fishing.

They can be cut into chunks for rays and bass, fillets for bass, turbot and brill, or the backbone can be removed to make a flapper for congers, bass and tope.

Keeping Them Fresh

If you're able to catch your own mackerel and want to keep some as bait for another day, you'll need to get them into a cool box packed with ice to keep them as fresh as possible. If you want to keep a lot of mackerel for bait, it pays to fillet them as soon as they're caught. Mackerel are oily fish and their flesh will start to break down as soon as they're dead, so put them in a zip-lock freezer bag and store in the ice; this way you can store fresh bait ready for future trips. Make sure you put them straight into the freezer as soon as you get home, though.

Mackerel make superb bait for most sea fish, and they're good to eat.

How To Bait Up With Mackerel

1 When the mackerel are 'in', even the youngsters can bag up as the fish come in close to the beach.

2 Small strips of mackerel are great for tempting black bream, gurnards, garfish and mackerel.

3 When taking a fillet off, always cut away from your fingers.

4 A fillet mounted like this is perfect for brill, turbot, bass and rays.

5 A whole mackerel can be mounted on a Pennel rig and cast from the shore for congers and bull huss.

6 A mackerel flapper is one of the top baits for congers, tope and sharks.

The Stop Knot

Learn how to tie the stop knot, which has several applications that can enhance your sea angling.

The stop knot is the match angler's favourite because it allows the fisherman to build an effective trace with few components.

Most importantly it allows the angler to move the snood up and down the trace, should that be required, without damaging the trace's body. The stop knot can also be used for preventing bait from sliding up the snood and away from the hook when casting, as well as setting the bait depth when float fishing.

Many anglers prefer to use Powergum for tying stop knots, which is a very stretchy and soft line. It's not at all suitable for use as a normal running line and is specially designed for its job.

However, it's just as easy and cheaper to tie stop knots with normal monofilament – just as long as it's the same diameter or heavier than the line that it's being tied to. The advantage of using mono is that it stays in place better, whereas Powergum can occasionally slip.

TopTips

1 Use saliva to lubricate the knot when tightening.

2 You can tie it with Powergum or monofilament.

3 Some anglers cut off a section of line to make the knot, but tying it from the tag end and trimming it after forming it will dramatically reduce any waste.

4 If using stop knots to secure snoods in place, it's best to tie one above the top-snood bead and two below the lower-snood bead. This is because a single stop knot under tension can slip. Tying two will prevent this.

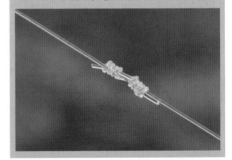

How To Tie The Stop Knot

1 Run the tag end of the stop-knot line alongside the snood/trace body and form a loop.

2 Make five turns through the loop with the tag end, ensuring you pass the tag around both the stop-knot line and the snood/trace body.

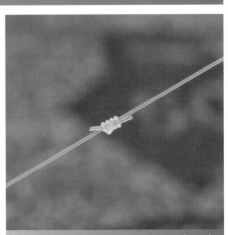

3 Now lubricate the knot, pull it up tight and trim off the tag ends.

Three-Hook Clipped-Down RIG

History Of The Rig

The three-hook rig has been around in different forms since the late 19th century and the modern three-hook flapper rig was designed with the hook snoods in sequence on a vertical rig body. It only really became popular when shore competition angling started to increase in popularity during the early 1970s, when anglers wanted to target multiple fish and use varied baits.

The invention of the bait clip came about in the late 1960s due to the revolution of long-range casting. Again in the early 1970s, the three-hook flapper evolved further to be used regularly with bait clips to streamline the baits and rig during the cast to gain distance and put three baits out to maximum range.

Since that time the three-hook clipped-down rig has become one of our most consistent rigs, and should be one of the first that the newcomer to sea angling learns to tie.

How It Works

Prior to casting, position the arm of the bait clip in the gape or bend of the hook. Now slide the bait clip down the rig body until the hook trace tightens. Do this with all three hook snoods and the rig is ready for casting.

When the lead weight hits the sea at the end of the cast, the main line and rig body will lose tension and fall slack. As it does so, the hooks slide free of the bait clips, leaving the baits and hook snoods to flow out into the tide as the rig settles on the sea bed.

If you find that the clips are not releasing it will be because you have kept a tight line between the rod and the rig until after the lead weight hits the water. This often happens to inexperienced anglers when there is a strong side wind, the wind pressure keeping the line taut. To get reliable bait-clip release, the rig body and line must fall fully slack as the lead weight hits the water.

The rubber stop and sequins act as a physical stop to avoid the bait blowing back up the hook snood and sliding up above the hook during the cast due to air pressure. The rubber rig stops can be slid up or down to suit different sizes of bait. To concentrate bait just on the hook, have the stop tight to the eye of the hook. If you want to slide a full-length worm onto the hook and up onto the snood, then slide the stop up the snood accordingly.

TopTip

If you're fishing in surf conditions, ideally use fluorocarbon line for the hook snoods because this is stiffer than mono and tangles less as the bait tumbles in the surf tables or swell.

The rig is ideal for targeting flounders, dabs, plaice, whiting, rockling, school bass, small codling, coalfish and dogfish, but will catch anything and everything on its day.

Build Sequence

1 Start with 54 inches of 60lb mono and tie on a Gemini lead link at one end.

2 Slide on a bait clip, a 3mm bead and a rig crimp. Now slide on a rig crimp, a 3mm rig bead, a size 10 rolling rig swivel, another rig bead and a crimp. Leave these loose for now.

3 Repeat this sequence twice more, then complete the rig with a strong size 4 rig-connector rolling swivel.

4 The first hook-trace swivel needs to be crimped one inch below the rig-connector swivel. The middle swivel should be about 18 inches down from the rig-connector swivel and the third crimped in place 32 inches down from it.

5 The top hook trace needs to be the longest at 15 inches, the second measures 13 inches, and the bottom one is the shortest at just 10 inches. Use 20lb fluorocarbon or clear mono line.

6 Slide a rubber rig stop and sequin onto each tied hook snood to form a bait stop and finish by tying on a Kamasan B940 Aberdeen size 2 or similar pattern hook.

7 Lastly, place each hook into the bait clip below and slide the bait clip up or down until the hook snood pulls just tight. Leave at least a ½in gap between the top of the bait clip, then crimp and secure the crimp in place. This gap allows the clip to slide upwards a little during casting, eliminating hook-snood stretch.

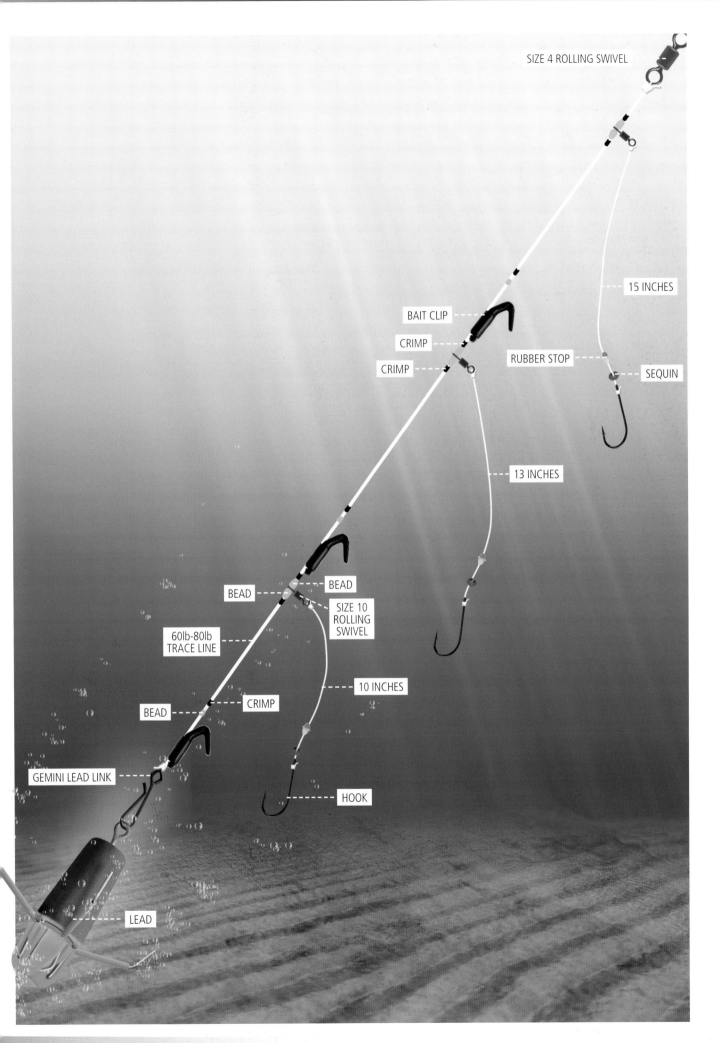

SIZE 4 ROLLING SWIVEL

15 INCHES

BAIT CLIP

CRIMP

CRIMP

RUBBER STOP

SEQUIN

13 INCHES

BEAD

BEAD

SIZE 10 ROLLING SWIVEL

60lb-80lb TRACE LINE

10 INCHES

BEAD

CRIMP

GEMINI LEAD LINK

HOOK

LEAD

EUROPE'S TOP FISHING MAGAZINES ARE AVAILABLE ON YOUR iPHONE, iPAD OR ANDROID DEVICE. . .

SIMPLY SEARCH THE RELEVANT MAGAZINE TITLE

(ALL THE FEATURES, NO PAPER CUTS)

ALSO LIVE ON THE ANDROID MARKET!

Shore Dabs

Grab your gear, catch more **dabs** and look like a shore fishing expert with this must-read guide.

Many anglers have trouble identifying dabs from other flatfish, especially plaice and flounders. The dab is visually unique, though. It has eyes on its right-hand side, like plaice and most flounders, but the lateral line distinctly curves sharply above the pectoral fin. The skin tends to be a fawny brown, which is sometimes mottled, but with pale, yellow misshapen spots. It also feels rough towards the head, whereas plaice and flounders feel smooth.

The dab's diet consists mainly of small worms, crabs, small shellfish and shrimps, but it is also predatory when fully adult and will take small sandeels, sprats and other small fish.

It is common throughout the whole of the UK, and found well north in the arctic waters around Iceland and off the Norwegian coast. It can tolerate depths from just a few inches on surf beaches at night, right down to 200 metres.

The dab's typical habitat is clean sand or mud, and sometimes fine shingle, with it mostly favouring areas of broken shell and mussel beds at the mouths of river estuaries.

The dab spawns between late March and June out in deeper water. It tends to be one of the last species to leave for spawning in the early spring period, returning as late as June.

When And Where

Dabs are common for most of the year off surf beaches and inside clean-ground harbours that offer a constant depth. They can also be caught in summer, but these tend to be small juvenile fish and are rarely targeted by anglers.

The main angling season runs from October when the bigger fish, which have been out in

Build A Three-Hook Shore-Dab Rig

1 Begin with 54 inches of 60lb mono. Go for a semi-supple type such as Sufix or the new Penn shockleader line. Tie on a Gemini lead link at one end using a five-turn grinner knot.

2 Slide on a rig crimp, a 3mm oval rig bead, a size 10 swivel, another rig bead and a crimp. Repeat this sequence to give you three full sets of crimps, beads and swivels. Leave these loose for now.

3 Complete the rig body with a size 4 rolling swivel, again using a five-turn grinner knot.

4 The first hook-trace swivel is placed one inch above the Gemini lead link. The middle swivel should be exactly 17 inches below the top swivel, which is one inch below the connector swivel.

5 The top hook trace needs to be 15 inches, the second trace 13 inches, and the bottom just 10 inches long. Ideally use 20lb fluorocarbon for its slight stiffness, but clear mono is okay.

6 Finish by sliding on a single 5mm luminous bead onto each hook trace and tie on a size 2 Kamasan B940 hook. Dabs are inquisitive fish and will home in on the luminous bead.

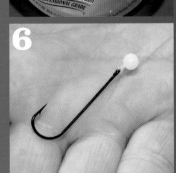

colder, deeper water, move back inshore as the sea temperature begins to drop. Numbers of dabs increase in most areas until Christmas, with the very biggest fish staying inshore and feeding well throughout January and February. By late February to early March their numbers reduce as they move offshore to spawn.

On surf beaches the best time to fish during the smaller neap tides is either side of low water. This will see you casting to fish that are resident in a more constant depth of water.

Usually on surf beaches they stay beyond the low-water line and won't push inshore with the flooding tide as it's too shallow.

On bigger spring tides they move inshore with the new flood, letting the tide bring them over fresh feeding ground, but they're rarely in among the surf tables. They commonly work the deeper water at medium casting range, so the casting distance can be important to maintain good catches.

On surf beaches, night always gives the best catches as the fish feed more confidently. The exception can be in coloured water after a blow, when a decent cast into deeper water will find dabs feeding eagerly.

Inside harbours and off breakwaters where the depth exceeds 15 feet, the dabs will feed throughout the daylight hours, although again catches will increase come nightfall.

Tackle
In calmer seas when the fish are at medium range up to 80 yards away, a bass rod capable of casting 2oz to 4oz matched to a lightweight fixed-spool reel carrying 12lb braid or mono plus 40lb shockleader – or a 5500C type multiplier – will give good sport. At closer range you can even use spinning rods for maximum sport with a smaller fixed-spool reel such as the Penn Sargus 4000 or Shimano equivalent.

When the fish are at a longer range, change to a standard 4oz to 6oz beachcaster. Reels such as the ABU 6500 or Daiwa 7HT series are good choices with 12lb to 15lb line and a 60lb-plus shockleader.

Bait
Fresh lug is good bait, but leave it in the shed to perish and become smelly and it will be even better!

Sand clams are another dab favourite. The top dab bait, however, is sticky black lug. This is gutted black lug deliberately left exposed to damp air so that it starts to dry out a little but goes sticky to the touch – and, most importantly, it stinks!

To prepare these, lay the lug out on newspaper and leave them open to the air during wet weather in a damp garage or shed until sticky. This bait will outfish all others in most conditions.

Other consistent dab baits are small sections of razorfish, small whole sand clams, mackerel strips, herring, small chunks of sandeel, squid strips, bluey strips and small chunks of peeler crab. Either side of Christmas, to target the biggest dabs try using a small strip of sprat bound onto the hook with elastic.

5 TopTips For Dabs

1 Dabs prefer baits presented hard on the sea bed. When fishing with three-hook rigs, fish a slightly slack line and watch the bow in the line for lifting to indicate a bite. A slack line guarantees that all the baits are on the sea bed.

2 On surf beaches look for lateral gullies and deeper holes, which pretty much always feature on this type of beach. These depressions and gullies need only be a few inches deep but will concentrate food and bring the dabs in.

3 Look for wooden groynes and fish your baits tight in to the end of them at low water and you'll see deep depressions where the tide scours out the sand. Food will collect here and so too will the dabs and other fish.

4 Dabs have small mouths; they can swallow big baits if left long enough, but using smaller hooks will catch you far more fish. You would normally use a size 2 dab hook, but using a size 4 or 6 and reducing the bait size can pay dividends.

5 Dabs advance up the beach with the flooding tide, so use a light, plain or flat lead and let the lateral-tide pressure on the line slowly drag the bait to cover much more ground than a fixed lead can – this can improve the catch rate.

How To Use
Razorfish

Sharpen your bait knowledge with this easy-to-follow guide.

Razorfish get their name because they look similar to the old-fashioned cut-throat razors. There are two types. The common razorfish is the larger of the two, growing up to 12 inches long with a fairly straight shell. The smaller sword razorfish has a curved shell and only grows to about six inches.

They live along the low waterline and the beds can extend way out to sea in depths of up to 100 feet. They prefer to live in fine, firmly packed sand rather than coarse sand that is continually moving. You can collect them on low spring tides by either digging with a fork – hard work – or with a container of salt or a salt-and-water mix.

They're quite easy to find once you get the hang of it. Simply look for little key-shaped holes in the sand, pour the salty water in and wait for the razor to emerge. When an inch or two of the

Razorfish – fresh or frozen – make good bait for many species.

shell appears, take a firm hold and pull gently until it releases its grip. If you pull too fast you'll lose the foot or be left with an empty shell.

Razorfish can be collected all year round but will burrow deeper during frosty spells, as worms and other

marine creatures do, to avoid the cold.

They make excellent bait for many species, such as cod, bass, bream and flatfish, and can be used whole, in bunches or in smaller pieces in a cocktail with worms and can be frozen down for future sessions.

How To Bait Up With Razorfish

1 Open the shell and slide the flesh out with your finger.

2 Thread the hook through the foot as if it was a worm.

3 Once you've threaded it on the hook, make sure the hook point is showing.

4 Bind it securely to the hook with fine elastic.

5 Once bound on, it can be cast a long way and will withstand small fish nibbling at it.

6 It can also be used to make up juicy cocktails with rag and crab.

The Spider Hitch
Shockleader Knot

How To Tie The Spider Hitch Knot

1 Form a 12in loop in the running line.

2 Make a loop on top of your index finger and grip tight.

3 Wind the loop around your finger four times and pass through the loop.

4 Moisten with saliva then slowly pull the tag loop tight and the loops will come off one at a time.

5 Push the coils together and slowly pull tight with steady pressure.

Learn how to tie one of the strongest shockleader knots around.

When attaching a 60lb to 80lb leader line to the running line it's essential that you tie a knot that doesn't weaken the running line too much.

Quite often it's the leader knot that's the weakest link in your setup. A badly tied knot will break way below the running line's stated breaking strain and, in some cases, a 15lb line could be reduced to a mere 6lb to 7lb breaking strain! This is a complete disaster and will regularly result in lost gear as well as your entire leader length.

Providing it's tied correctly, the spider hitch has as close to 100 per cent strength as a leader knot can have.

A strong knot will ensure that you don't lose fish, tackle or your temper, and will result in more time spent fishing and less time retying leaders!

How To Attach The Spider To The Leader

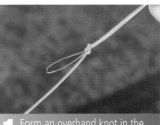

1 Form an overhand knot in the leader and pass the spider loop through about an inch or so, then tighten fully.

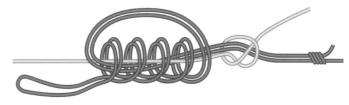

2 Lubricate the running line and slide the two knots together.

3 Create the smallest uni knot you can by using four turns and lubricate.

4 Push the coils together and tighten by applying steady pressure on both the leader line and running line. Trim the tags.

Two-Hook Leger/Drift RIG

History Of The Rig

This rig is one of few that are equally effective fished from the shore and the boat. It's one of the traditional rigs that have been in use since the late 1800s, though it has undergone major changes with regard to components. It was often quoted as 'the' flatfish rig from the turn of the 20th century up until the mid-1960s, and was commonly used over top turbot marks such as the Shambles Bank, off Weymouth.

It's still a good rig for shore flatfish, as well as rays, dogfish and even bass. From the boat it's useful for basic drift fishing when after whiting, flatfish, gurnards and rays – plus match anglers like it when targeting dogfish for points.

How It Works

Off the shore the rig is good for short to medium-range fishing. The lower hook trace sits hard on the sea bed and will target the true bottom feeders such as flatfish and rays. However, the top hook can be fished to either a tight line to keep the bait moving just off the bottom targeting free swimmers, such as bass, whiting, coalies and codling, or a semi-slack line to put both baits on the sea bed to give a maximum scent trail when after dogs and rays.

This rig is also useful for fishing at close quarters down the side of breakwaters, harbour walls and jetties. You'll be fishing a vertical line mostly in these circumstances with the lower hook targeting bottom species and the top hook finding the free-swimming fish.

It works in much the same way off the boat. You can fish it as an uptiding rig, with the bow in the line keeping both hook baits hard on the sea bed taking all manner of species, including cod and rays.

It's also a great rig for drift fishing. The lower hook will drag across the sea bed attracting dabs, plaice, gurnards, whiting and codling – with the top hook bouncing the bait up off the sea bed depending on how much line you let out.

With a steep line angle the top hook is up in the water, but with a shallow line angle – for example, when fishing far out – both baits are on the sea bed.

This is also a great haddock rig and can be particularly successful over mixed ground such as off the west coast of Ireland where you'll find a huge variety of species.

Having the two hooks also means that you can fish two different baits to target different types of fish at once – say a crab bait for bass and a worm bait for flatties.

You can also fish one big bait and one small bait to target whatever fish come through.

When fishing in among mixed rough ground, change the snoods to a line with a breaking strain of less than your main line – so, should the hooks snag, the snoods will break away, preserving your rig. You can also attach the lead weight by a weak link of phone wire or lighter line to achieve the same result should the weight snag when on the drift.

Build Sequence

1 Start with a size 4 rolling swivel and tie on 12 inches of 60lb clear mono.

2 To the end of the mono tie on a size 4 three-way swivel by an end eye.

3 To the other end eye tie on 20 inches of 60lb clear mono.

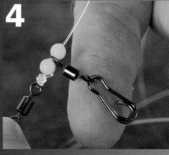

4 Slide on a 5mm bead, a size 4 link swivel by the connector eye, another 5mm bead, then tie on a size 4 rolling swivel. The link swivel takes the lead weight.

5 The top hook trace is 10 inches of 25lb fluorocarbon or clear mono tied to the middle eye of the three-way swivel. The lower hook trace is 12 inches of the same line.

6 For flatfish use Kamasan B940 Aberdeens size 2, or Mustad Aberdeen Match equivalents. For dogfish use size 1/0 hooks, and for rays and bass size 3/0 Mustad Viking patterns.

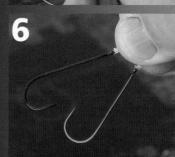

You can attach your main line direct to the top of the three-way swivel to eliminate the top swivel, but its preferable not to because the extra swivel minimises line twist.

THREE-WAY SWIVEL

SNOOD

SIZE 4 SWIVEL

BEAD BEAD

HOOK

SNOOD

HOOK

LEAD LINK

SWIVEL

LEAD

Lubing A Multiplier

Many anglers are afraid to lube the bearings on their multiplier for fear of not being able to put it back together. But, in practice, it's dead simple…

All mechanical things need maintenance and lubrication, especially your reels, which take a lot of abuse throughout a session. Oil not only lubricates your bearings, its viscosity (or thickness) helps control the spool's revolutions during a cast. It pays to have two or three different grades of oil for different conditions. For example, you can use thinner oil during winter and thicker oil in summer when the heat will thin it.

The first thing to do is slacken the screws on the handle side and remove the side plate; you can then slide the spool off the spindle. The next step is to remove the circlip that holds the bearing in place and slide the bearing out of the housing.

Wash out the old oil from the bearing with petrol, lighter fuel or a solvent such as clutch and brake cleaner – but please do not do this near a naked flame or while smoking!

Once you've cleaned the bearing, leave it on a piece of kitchen towel until all the solvent has evaporated; you can then add a couple of drops of reel oil to relubricate.

Slide the bearings back in the spool housing and replace the circlips carefully. Then, once you have reassembled the reel, you're all set to go.

How To Oil The Bearings

1 Carefully remove the circlip.

2 Slide the bearing out of the spool.

3 Flush the old oil out with petrol or a solvent.

4 Lay the bearing on a piece of kitchen towel until all the petrol or solvent has evaporated, then…

5 … add a couple of drops of oil.

6 Put the bearings and circlips back in the spool and reassemble the reel.

The Albright Knot

Learn how to join braided lines to monofilament.

The reason we need to join braid and mono lines is because braid has no stretch and a low abrasion resistance, so we counter this by attaching a mono leader to act as a shock absorber and rubbing line.

The problem is that braid and mono are very different in their properties and are particularly hard to join by using standard knots, since the braid can easily slip away from the mono – but the Albright is the solution to this. The main application for this knot is for boat fishing.

TopTips

1 Use saliva to lubricate the knot when tightening.

2 Be careful not to nick the lines when trimming up.

3 Should the knot slip, make more turns when creating it to lock it off.

How To Tie The Albright Knot

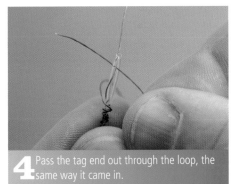

1 Form a loop in the monofilament – try to squeeze it to a rough point.

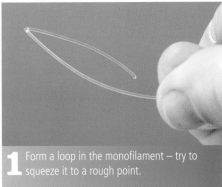

2 Pass the braid through the loop and make eight turns downwards.

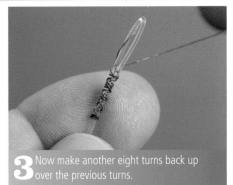

3 Now make another eight turns back up over the previous turns.

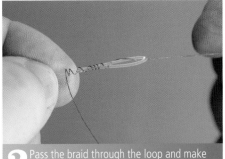

4 Pass the tag end out through the loop, the same way it came in.

5 Slowly pull the coils up by pulling both the braid and the running line.

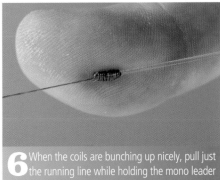

6 When the coils are bunching up nicely, pull just the running line while holding the mono leader until it's tightened. Trim the tags and that's it!

Learn How To
Cast Bait Further

Top angler and caster **Peter Thain** explains how you can cast baits 'over the horizon' in a safe and controlled way…

Fishing has been so much more fun since I learnt to cast further. I don't use the technique every time I fish because on many occasions the fish are close in and it would be foolish to cast straight over the top of them. But, when the wind is in your face and you still need to get bait out there, it's good to be able to turn up the power on demand.

This cast is my fishing pendulum, it uses much less power than I would use in competition casting. Power should always be kept down to a safe level on the beach when there are other people around. Always remember that you go fishing to catch fish. If you want to try to cast as far as you can, then go to a tournament where it will be appreciated.

The Beginning...

Using a clock face is an easy way to understand where everything should be at the start of the cast. Imagine that straight out to sea is 12 o'clock, and straight back up the beach is six o'clock. You are standing in the middle of the clock face.

I start each cast in exactly the same way. I begin by first setting the drop at the correct length. My preferred drop length places the lead besides my upper rod hand (the drop is the amount of shockleader you have outside the rod tip, between the tip ring and the lead). In the start position my feet are a comfortable shoulder width apart, and I'm facing three o'clock. I take a small step back with my left foot, and then place most of my weight on the right foot. Rotating from the hips, I turn my upper body until the rod is pointing towards eight o'clock. I'm now in a position to start swinging the lead, and I want it to swing away from me towards eight o'clock.

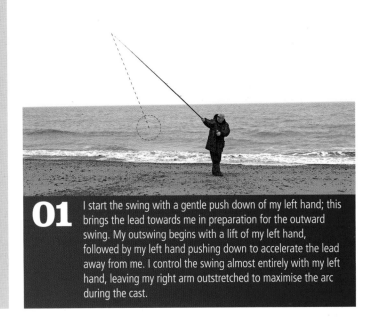

01 I start the swing with a gentle push down of my left hand; this brings the lead towards me in preparation for the outward swing. My outswing begins with a lift of my left hand, followed by my left hand pushing down to accelerate the lead away from me. I control the swing almost entirely with my left hand, leaving my right arm outstretched to maximise the arc during the cast.

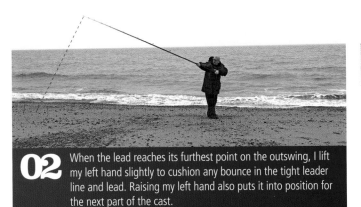

02 When the lead reaches its furthest point on the outswing, I lift my left hand slightly to cushion any bounce in the tight leader line and lead. Raising my left hand also puts it into position for the next part of the cast.

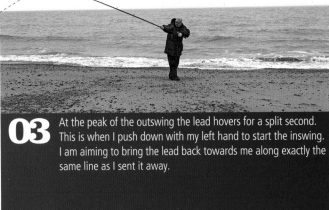

03 At the peak of the outswing the lead hovers for a split second. This is when I push down with my left hand to start the inswing. I am aiming to bring the lead back towards me along exactly the same line as I sent it away.

04 A relatively small push downwards with my left hand is all that's needed to get the lead coming back towards me. I keep a nice steady pace in the swing. Too slow and the lead will lack enough momentum to get into the right place. Too fast and I will spend the rest of the cast trying to catch up to the lead before I can begin to bend the rod.

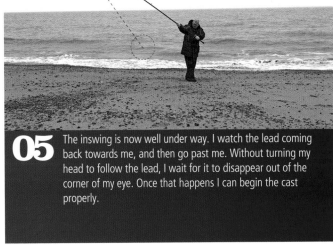

05 The inswing is now well under way. I watch the lead coming back towards me, and then go past me. Without turning my head to follow the lead, I wait for it to disappear out of the corner of my eye. Once that happens I can begin the cast properly.

06 Once the lead disappears from the corner of my eye, my left hand begins to rise into position to bring the rod around. By lifting my left hand I also change the path of the lead from an upward trajectory to a horizontal one.

07 The lead is now travelling on a slightly climbing horizontal plane, and my left foot is moving across in a step. I'm going to plant my left foot so that both feet are at roughly 45 degrees to the direction of the cast. This further winds the muscles in my torso up, and extends the amount of time they are effective. It also provides a very stable base from which to deliver the cast. Note that the rod has hardly moved at all.

08 The step across is now complete, both feet are on the ground and the weight is still over my right foot. I've started to unwind my body in sequence from bottom to top, starting with the hips. You can see the rod still hasn't moved a great deal and the lead is continuing to track along a gently climbing horizontal plane.

09 I'm slowly unwinding my body to accelerate the lead, which has reached its peak height and is on its descent. Only when it's close to its lowest point can I apply the power. My body weight is still mainly on my right foot. There has been no real effort in the cast so far – I'm using body rotation to generate effortless power. The positioning of the lead from the inswing does the rest of the work for me.

10 With the lead near its lowest point, I finally apply some power to the cast. This drags the lead back upwards, and generates even more bend in the rod. I complete the cast by simultaneously driving off my right foot, unwinding the rest of my body, and pulling in hard with my left hand. My right hand does little work – the majority of force comes from the left.

11 It's the end of the cast and the lead is now heading out to sea. I'm still in a braced position against my left leg to prevent any further rotational movement and give a clean release. Failure to stop the rotation effectively causes surge problems on a multiplier and ring wraps with a fixed-spool reel.

North Norway

WORLD'S BEST SEA FISHING

The No.1 destination - all year round

In the Summer... fish where the sun never sets!

Our midnight sun fishing packages developed over the last ten years are a sell out year on year. From May to early August the sun never sets – its 24 hours a day daylight!

In the Winter... fish under the Northern Lights

We have now developed some special, extreme Monster Cod spring trips, our biggest cod this spring was 73 pounds 8 ounces!

Booking early is the only way to secure your place to some of the best sea fishing in the world, stunning scenery and the most amazing catches on earth. Huge cod, prolific natural stocks, massive halibut, plus great fishing for big coalfish, wolfish and plaice.

Excellent accommodation and boats, both self use and skippered all amidst beautiful scenery.

Our holiday locations are great for the serious sea angler and those taking partners/families.

All our holidays are financially protected.

Anglers World Holidays

BOOK NOW FOR 2012
01246 221717

www.anglersworld.tv

ABTA BONDED for your financial protection

ABTA
42639

Get Hooked on Fishing...

Building Positive Futures

All coaches are UKCC qualified and disclosure checked

GHOF BTEC classroom session

Peer Mentoring

WHAT DO WE DO ?

We work with local communities to help create opportunities for young people.

We deliver fun and interactive training around the sport of angling. Our programme is especially designed with the help of young people to give the participants more confidence and to demonstrate that there are alternative pathways and better opportunities available to them.

We help to train and develop peer mentors at the same time as encouraging young people to take an active part in how we run the local schemes.

We are happy to work with all young people aged 6 and over and have a proven track-record in delivering social inclusion, improvements in school attendance and educational achievement.

Learning about sharks !

" **Most Youth Service professionals who have encountered the Get Hooked on Fishing scheme have sensed something special about the project. There is an apparent synergy of vision, commitment, process and tangible outcomes.** "

(Home Office - Positive Futures) **substance.**

HOW YOU CAN HELP US...

"As a registered Charity, Get Hooked on Fishing relies on donations to carry out it's work. In 2010 we helped over 5500 young people through our intervention programmes - we hope to do more in 2011. Any help you can give would be greatly appreciated, so why not go online now and make a donation - help us to help them."

Get Hooked on Fishing- they both did !

so help us to help them at :

www.ghof.org.uk

LOTTERY FUNDED

Get Hooked on Fishing

Get Hooked on Fishing is a charity registered in Scotland (SCO 040038) and in England and Wales (1132448) and is a company limited by guarantee (0680071)

Shore Thornback Rays

Rays offer great sport from the shore and are easy to target. We show you how to get the best action this season.

Rays make up one of the more difficult groups of fish to identify individually, as thornbacks, spotted and small-eyed rays can be caught over the same ground. Just to confuse things further, blonde rays can also be caught off the shore alongside thornbacks over certain types of ground.

Identification And Facts

Rays that are covered across the back with small and defined spots are spotted and blonde rays. Small-eyed rays have white or creamy white blotches and lines running across their backs. The thornback has a short but more pointed nose than the other rays and the angles of the outer wing are at right angles to each other. Thornbacks are, to a greater or lesser extent, covered with thorns across the wings, whereas the other rays tend to have their thorns concentrated down their spines, tails and lightly at the forward edges of the wings.

Their coloration on the back is more greyish brown when living on mud, to fawn or sandy brown when on sand with a white/grey belly. Occasionally thornbacks have dark, eye-shaped roundels on the middle of each wing, and some will show a mixed mottling of fawn and darker-brown shades.

Thornbacks breed in the period from January to May. Female rays move into weed beds and reef areas to deposit their eggs among the weed and stones. The eggs are housed in egg sacs often referred to as 'mermaid's purses'. These are a common find when walking along the shoreline after the eggs have hatched.

The embryos take from 16 to 20 weeks to hatch and the newly hatched, 3¼in-wide fish will feed on small shrimps and amphipods.

As adults their diet consists of shrimps, numerous types of crab, and small fish such as poor cod, whiting, flatfish and sandeels. When living close to the shore, thornback rays will also move very close in after a heavy storm to feed on broken clams, mussels, razorfish and lugworms.

How To Build A One-Hook Clipped-Down Ray Rig

1 Start with a 30in length of 60lb rig-body line. Tie on a Gemini lead link at the base.

2 Slide on a Breakaway Impact shield followed by a bead and a crimp. Position it just above the link knot and secure the crimp in place, leaving about an inch for the shield to slide in.

3 Slide on a rig crimp, a rig bead, a small rig swivel, another bead and a crimp. Leave these loose for now. Then, to the remaining free end of 60lb line, add a strong size 4 rig-body swivel.

4 The hook trace is a 24in length of 30lb fluorocarbon or, alternatively, 40lb mono. Slide on a size 5mm bead, then finish with a Viking 79515 size 3/0 hook.

5 Above the bead on the hook snood, tie in a Powergum stop knot to form a bait stop to prevent the bait blowing back up the hook snood during the cast or on impact with the water.

6 Locate the hook in the Impact Shield and slide the rig, bead and swivel assembly up the trace until the hooklength comes just tight, then secure the rig crimps in place.

Thornbacks tend to swim in small groups of three to seven fish. Typically there'll be one or two females and three or four smaller males. If you catch one ray, you're more than likely to catch more in quick succession.

When And Where To Fish

Thornbacks are found throughout the UK and Ireland. Their range also covers as far north as the southern coast of Iceland, up to the middle coastal region of Norway, and south encompassing the whole of the Mediterranean and the northern tip of Africa.

They are most common on our western-facing coasts, but the East Anglian beaches and Holderness beaches in south Yorkshire can also produce good numbers of rays at times.

These fish can be caught from shallow open beaches where they move in with the tide and sit in shallow gutters that run parallel with the beach where food gets deposited, or on the inclines of sandbanks where food is left by the tide.

They also move into the mouths of our smaller estuaries, again favouring sandbanks and deeper channels. Occasionally they can be caught inside larger harbours, when casting from breakwaters and harbour walls onto clean ground.

Other good marks are rock ledges that give access to deeper water over sand.

Long Range

On deeper beaches and rock ledges, thornbacks can be caught on any size of tide, but on the beaches it's mainly the bigger spring tides that produce the best results. The middle-sized tides rising towards the biggest spring tides are the best ones for consistent results. The rays move in with the new flood tide and will travel to the mid-tide level, generally, so long casting will often pay when after shallow beach rays. Also, try to pick a low tide that falls into dark.

The vast majority of rays from the shallow beaches will be caught in the hours of darkness – few are caught in daylight. Off the deeper watermarks, especially those over 50 feet, then daylight catches are more likely.

A good time to fish for thornies is directly after a storm when the sea is calming down and still coloured. Rays will move tight inshore to feed on food exposed by the scouring action of the waves.

Migration

There are two main inward migrations of thornbacks. One occurs in the spring triggered by the dropping of the egg sacs by the females and then breeding, but also by the first flush of peeling crabs along the shore. These fish stay close in until mid-June or so, and then move out once more.

A secondary migration occurs in September, coinciding with the big equinoctial tides. These fish move in with the whiting and they stay until late November in some areas.

Ray Tackle

Casting distance can be important to reach the rays, and to lift them up ledges when fishing deeper water. This requires a 12ft to 14ft 4oz to 6oz beachcaster with a fast, or ultra-fast, taper action.

Over clean sand, fast-running multipliers such as the ABU 6500i TSR or the Daiwa 7HT Mag loaded with 15lb line and a 60lb to 80lb shockleader will get good distance. If you prefer a fixed spool, go for a larger 8000 size and load it fully with line to maximise casting potential.

In areas where rays need to be brought back across mixed rough ground, and when fishing from deep-water ledges, then stronger reels such as the Penn 525Mag2 or ABU 7000 series have the gears and retrieves to bully big fish.

General Thornback Baits

One of the top baits is a mackerel/squid cocktail. This is simply a 3in by 1in strip of mackerel, with a strip of squid laid alongside it and bound up with bait elastic.

A 2in to 3in section of bluey is also good, as it gives off a huge amount of oil and will draw rays in. For extra attraction you can add squid.

A whole small to medium-sized squid is effective, as is a fillet of poor cod or pout. In spring, herring can be a real killer, especially when fresh.

In some areas large sandeels are prime baits for thornbacks, used whole by cutting the head and tail off, feeding the body up the hook and over the hook eye, then whipping in place with elastic leaving the hook point exposed.

Seasonal Bait

In spring peeler crab can be deadly when fishing off the beaches in close proximity to rougher ground.

In the autumn period a lot of thornbacks are caught on lug baits aimed at cod. Simply push two or thee lug up the shank of the hook and tip this with a strip of squid.

After storms thornies will also take razorfish, mussel and clam baits.

Get it right and you too could catch a fish like this 11½-pounder.

5 TopTips For Rays

1 Fishing two rods side by side is an advantage when targeting rays. By having two baits in the water in relatively near proximity, when you rebait or catch a fish, the other bait is left out there to keep a scent in the water and retains the interest of any other rays moving into the feeding area you've established.

4 The new short body 150g DVice is an excellent way to gain a little extra casting distance, plus it maintains good bait presentation. You can also cut up some small chunks of mackerel, literally just ¼in squares, and put a few of these into the base of the tube before you slide in the main hook bait. When the DVice hits the sea, out pops the bait followed by the small mackerel squares. These then drift downtide and act as groundbait.

2 If you think you may struggle to reach the rays you can use a technique called 'lining back'. This requires a big fixed-spool reel holding 300 yards plus of 15lb line – an 8000 size is ideal. Using chest waders, walk out into the surf as far as you can and cast out. As the tide floods in, keep releasing line as you walk back with the tide. Eventually your bait will be 200 yards out and in ray territory.

3 You should always study a beach at low water before you attempt to go fishing. Look for the deeper areas and parallel gutters, which will certainly hold any rays as they move inshore. In addition, watch the surf as it breaks – areas where the surf breaks less indicate deeper-water spots – these are the hotspots to try as the tide floods in.

5 In many areas, especially along the Holderness coast and off the Welsh coast, big shrimps, prawns and uncooked tiger prawns from the supermarket make great bait. Just slide the prawn up the hook tail, then place another one alongside it and secure with bait elastic.

PASSIONATE A

With seven specialist titles to choose from there's a magazine for every angler, no matter what your discipline.

It's so easy to subscribe too... check out our full range of titles and pick the one that best suits you — or that special someone you're treating — and place your order.

CarpFishing

Whether you've caught your first twenty or you simply want to catch much bigger fish, **Advanced Carp Fishing** is the magazine for you.

It's packed full of easy-to-read features, stunning photos and loads of top tips from the best carp anglers in the country.

www.advancedcarpfishing.com

matchfishing

Match Fishing is THE magazine to learn from. Covering all aspects of competition fishing — with in-depth features and stories from commercial fisheries and natural waters — no matter what your preference or level of ability, there is something for everyone to enjoy, every month, in Match Fishing!

www.matchfishingmagazine.com

Pole Fishing is the premier read for the angler who wants to learn more about pole fishing and the tackle used. With a team that is 100 per cent dedicated to showing you the best pole fishing tactics in an easy-to-read format, you're sure to have that red-letter day in the bag with our top advice.

www.polefishingmagazine.com

WE ARE TOO

Two-Hook Cascade RIG

History Of The Rig

This rig made an impact on the match scene just over a decade ago and is a modification of the one-up/one-down rig.

It was highly successful for several years, especially in the Kent and Sussex areas, and along the coast of North Wales, and is still popular today with match and pleasure anglers.

It came into being when Breakaway Tackle introduced its Cascade swivel. This is a normal swivel eye and body, but with the lower eye replaced with a loop of wire to take the hook-trace line, plus a stand-off clip that can hold a baited hook securely in position during the cast. This eliminated the need for a bait clip for the top hook and created a more streamlined rig, but with the advantage of having a long hook trace at both the top and bottom of the rig.

Too many anglers ignore this rig because it is a little fiddly to tie, and not overly easy to set up ready for casting, but it's a top rig and well worth mastering.

How It Works

The Cascade rig is particularly effective for plaice and flounders in daylight, and for scratching out pout, rockling and eels. Also try it at night for close to medium-range codling, school bass, coalfish and dabs. It can also account for surf turbot, which prefer baits that are allowed to move across the sand naturally with the ebb and flow of the passing surf.

The advantage, when fishing during daylight in gin-clear seas, is that it puts distance between the bait, the lead and the rig, meaning that shy fish are less likely to be spooked by movement of the rig body through wave action. Flashes of light reflecting off the clear rig body can be a deterrent for some fish when they're feeding in shallow depths.

It's also versatile. The lower hook trace is tight on the sea bed and appeals to flatfish and other species that have a preference for feeding hard on the bottom. The top hook trace, though, can be adjusted in the way it fishes just by raising and lowering the rod tip. By slackening the line we can have the top bait also sat on the

Build Sequence

1 Begin with a 56in length of 60lb clear rig-body line. At one end tie on a Gemini lead link

2 Slide on a Breakaway Impact Shield followed by a 3mm bead and a rig crimp.

3 Slide on another rig crimp, then a rig bead, a size 10 swivel, another rig bead and a crimp to take the bottom hook trace. Leave these loose for now.

4 Add another crimp, a bead, a swivel, a bead and a crimp assembly for the top hook trace. Finish the rig body with a size 4 swivel.

5 You'll find this rig easier to work with now if you hang the rig vertically on a hook using the top connector swivel and add a 5oz weight to the lead link to fully tighten the rig-body line.

6 Crimp the lower hook-trace swivel in place, but leave a good 2in gap for the Impact Shield to sit inside between the lead and the lower swivel crimp.

7 The lower hook trace is built in two halves and from clear mono. First tie on a 13in section of 20lb to 25lb line, then tie on a Breakaway Cascade swivel by the wire loop.

8 Add a 12in section of the 20lb to 25lb line to the eye of the Cascade swivel. Now slide on a rubber rig stop and a sequin to this lowest hook trace to act as a bait stop, then finish with a Kamasan B940 Aberdeen size 2 or 1.

9 The top hook trace is a single section of the 20lb to 25lb line about 30 inches long, with the rubber rig stop, sequin and Aberdeen size 2 hook added.

10 To set the rig up properly, position the hook on the lower hook trace into the Impact Shield ready for casting. This forms the hook trace into a long loop with the Cascade swivel in the middle of the loop formed. Clip the top hook into the Cascade swivel's wire release tag, and slide the top crimp assembly up the rig-body line until all comes tight, then crimp in position. This means that both hook traces are held tight with the hooks in the guard and Shield ready for casting, and the top hook is neatly clipped inside the Cascade swivel.

11 Finally, position the bead and crimp above the Impact Shield and crimp them in place. Make sure that the Impact Shield has a little room to slide in but not more than an inch, otherwise the Cascade swivel can release the top hook trace early and in flight.

How It Works Continued...

sea bed, appealing to the bottom feeders. But, by simply tightening the line between the rod tip and the rig, we then lift the bait up in the water and can have it dancing in the tide just off the bottom where it will appeal to the more mobile swimming fish such as bass, coalfish and codling.

Remember that this rig gives you another advantage when you're getting bites but not hooking many fish. This is typically around slack water when the tide run eases and fish can manoeuvre up to the bait at their leisure. Even if they

take the bait, without the tide run and if the fish is under 1lb in weight, there isn't enough tidal pressure adding weight to the fish to guarantee self-hooking. If this is the case, a switch to the Cascade rig can get you back to catching fish, simply because the length of the hook traces allows the fish to build up a little swimming speed before coming up hard against the hook, plus fish take a bait more confidently in shallow water with a long trace.

Having the hook traces split in two also allows you the opportunity to leave the 20lb to

25lb line as the first section, but then have the line direct to the hook trace made from a lighter line such as 12lb to 15lb. With the Impact Shield allowed to slide in that 2in gap, on casting, as the pressure of the cast stretches the rig-body line and also the hook traces, the Impact Shield will slide up, reducing the pressure but not allowing the hook to release prematurely. This means that you can utilise the lighter hook traces in clear, shallow seas and at times when you want maximum movement for natural appearance in your baits.

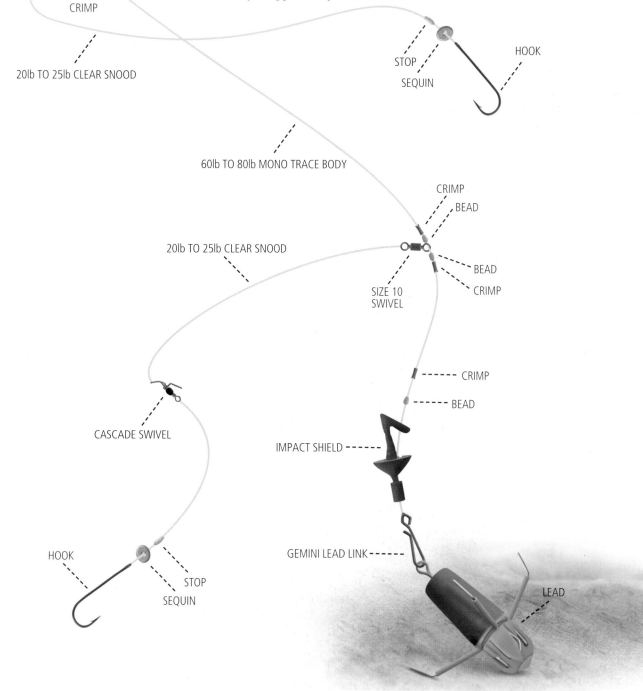

SIZE 4 SWIVEL

CRIMP

BEAD

SIZE 10 SWIVEL

BEAD

CRIMP

20lb TO 25lb CLEAR SNOOD

60lb TO 80lb MONO TRACE BODY

STOP

SEQUIN

HOOK

20lb TO 25lb CLEAR SNOOD

CRIMP

BEAD

BEAD

CRIMP

SIZE 10 SWIVEL

CRIMP

BEAD

CASCADE SWIVEL

IMPACT SHIELD

HOOK

STOP

SEQUIN

GEMINI LEAD LINK

LEAD

Boat Pollack

Pollack fight hard and fast, hit lures with a vengeance and offer the angler plenty of exciting sport. We show you how to get the very best from these sporting fish…

The pollack is relatively easy to identify, with it only sometimes being confused with the coalfish as both live over similar ground features and wrecks. The pollack's mouth is the key difference, with the lower lip being noticeably longer than the top lip, whereas the coalfish's lips are almost equal in length. Also, the pollack's lateral line above the pectoral fin curves in an upward direction, but on the coalfish this is straight.

The pollack is one of our hardest-fighting fish, with the ability to bore hard for the sea bed using its sleek, streamlined design and a big paddle tail for rapid bursts of acceleration. It has a big eye to maximise light intensity and uses this to chase down baitfish – typically attacking from below by silhouetting its prey against the surface light.

The pollack's diet consists mainly of launce sandeels, but it also eats scad, herring and mackerel in season. It's also happy to feed on the sea bed, taking small flatfish, whiting, codling, coalfish and other pollack too. At certain times, wreck-dwelling pollack become preoccupied with sprats and whitebait and are sometimes found to be full of shrimps.

Tackle

Modern pollack fishing tackle is getting lighter and lighter for maximum sport. Most anglers now choose a light 12lb to 15lb-class rod that's about 8ft 6in

Boat Pollack Flying-Collar Rig

1 Begin with a hollow-plastic boom; the longer 12in ones are best as they reduce the likelihood of tangles.

2 Thread the clear leader through the boom, slide on an 8mm bead and tie on a size 4 rolling swivel.

3 To the eye of the swivel tie on 12 feet of 15lb to 20lb fluorocarbon or clear mono line.

4 Cut the 12ft section of line in the middle and tie in a size 4 rolling swivel.

5 To the end of the flowing trace tie on a size 4/0 hook with a wide gape. Add a Berkley Power Worm pattern, artificial sandeel or shad.

6 To the link swivel on the bend of the boom, tie on a short weak link of mono line, then the lead. The weak link saves tackle and fish should the lead become snagged.

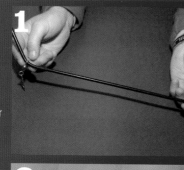

long with a supple tip but stiff butt section to maximise fighting power. They match these rods to a light multiplier such as the ABU Revo Toro Winch, or a 7000-sized multiplier from the Daiwa or Shimano stable. Braid has become the main choice for line, fished with a short 20ft leader of clear mono or fluorocarbon. Mono running line is okay but tends to need more lead weight than the braid; therefore reducing the sport gained from using light tackle.

In shallower reef situations, try fishing with a light 9ft to 9ft 6in spinning rod, 4000-sized fixed-spool reel and 15lb braided line with a short 15ft fluorocarbon shockleader of 20lb. The fish will really fight on this outfit and even a five-pounder will give a really good account of itself!

When And Where

The pollack is widespread throughout the UK but the species is most common on the west side of the British Isles. It is also found as far north as Iceland and the Trondheim Fjord in Norway.

The pollack's habitat is largely among rocky reef ground both inshore and offshore. It typically lives around steeply rising rock pinnacles, using the structure to break the tide run. Baitfish shoals also use the same structure for protection, so it's good hunting ground for the predatory fish.

The Cornish reefs, Wales and the west coast of Scotland offer excellent pollack sport, but Ireland has some of the best fishing along both its southern and west-facing coastlines where deep water and reef ground mix.

If you want to target the very biggest pollack then you need to fish the deep-water wrecks in depths from 200 to 350 feet. Here the pollack will adjust its height in the water column to suit both the tide run and the availability of food. Wrecks in the English Channel consistently produce specimen fish, as do wrecks in the Irish Sea off Wales and the wrecks off the southern coast of Ireland.

Pollack can be caught throughout the year, but the reef fishing is best in autumn, from late August through to mid-November in most areas. It's then that the bigger fish are feeding up prior to spawning and will be more concentrated in numbers.

On the wrecks the biggest fish – these being females – show through mid-January to early April. The fish are getting ready for spawning at this time and will feed heavily, meaning that they compete more with the smaller fish for food, making them more likely to be caught by anglers.

Use light tackle for the best sport.

5 TopTips For Pollack

1 When using artificial shads or worms, the colour is crucial on the day, and the fish's preference can even change by the hour. Experienced anglers tend to choose a black lure first, especially one with a black body and a bright-red or orange tail referred to as a firetail. The black body will give a good silhouette for the attacking fish, but it has that brighter-coloured tail that will often trigger an aggressive response from predatory fish. Red and blue are also consistent fish takers.

When using weighted and non-weighted shads you'll find that the smaller 4in size will take far more fish than the bigger 5in – a fact that many anglers seem to disregard.

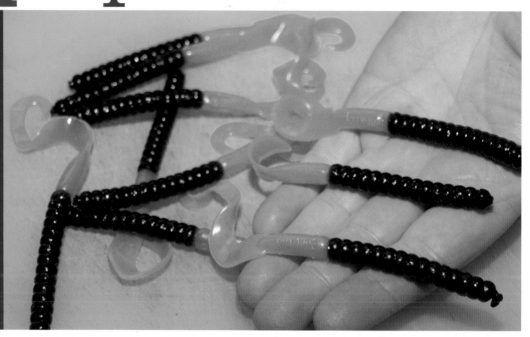

2 Both wreck and reef-dwelling pollack will lift in the water column when the tide run is easing and the swimming becomes easier. As the tide flow increases they drop back deeper and seek out sheltered areas behind rocks and wrecks to save energy.

Count the turns of the reel handle to gauge depth, noting how many turns it takes on average to find feeding fish. A line-counter reel is an excellent option.

3 When working a lure, allow it to descend slowly to the sea bed, then as you feel the 'tap' of the lead weight touching bottom, click the reel into gear and begin a slow, steady retrieve. Count up to 25 turns of the reel handle, then drop the lure back to the sea bed and start a new retrieve. Vary the speed of retrieve from time to time to gauge what the fish want on the day, because this can differ. Occasionally adding a burst of speed to a lure will induce an attack from an otherwise disinterested fish.

The pollack eats its prey by sucking it in. On the rod tip you'll feel a gradual increase in pressure as the line slowly tightens. It is important that you continue the slow retrieve and do not strike. As the pollack fully engulfs the lure it will turn back towards the wreck or reef and hook itself.

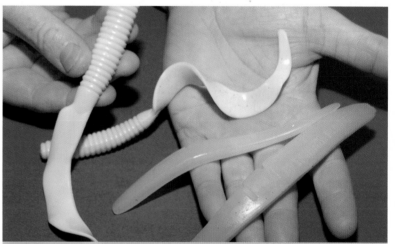

4 In slightly coloured water, evident after prolonged bad weather, it pays to use a lure of a bright colour, such as orange or yellow. These obviously stand out better in the coloured water. At depth in these conditions, luminous yellow or green lures can also work well, and using a camera flash to ignite the luminescence can dramatically increase their effectiveness.

5 Instead of lure fishing, try a live launce sandeel. Allow the launce to drift over the reef or wreck just above the structure, or try a very slow retrieve upwards through the water column. Where the tide run is light, you can also trot a freelined sandeel over the edge of the reef in a downtide direction. The pollack will sit behind the reef and wait to pounce on small sandeels and baitfish that get washed over the edge, so this is a highly effective method that's capable of producing big bags of fish.

Kayak Safety

With kayak angling becoming more popular than ever, we've put together an essential safety guide for any budding paddling piscators.

Safety

There are two kinds of safety...

1 Primary safety. This is where your own decisions and actions keep you out of trouble. For example, you decide whether it is safe to go out depending on what the weather is like. This is the best option.

2 Secondary safety. This is where primary safety has failed or is not applicable and you use your knowledge, equipment and techniques to solve a problem or get out of a situation that has occurred. Things do go wrong and sometimes there is very little you can do about it other than to minimise the risk, mitigate the circumstances and manage the incident, which could include calling for outside assistance.

ALL the kit is of secondary importance, compared with the initial decision of whether to launch or not. If the conditions are borderline for your current experience, then do not launch – if the conditions worsen while you are on the water, you are likely to find yourself beyond your capabilities.

If going in a group, the group should paddle in conditions suited to the least experienced member of the group. Expanding your knowledge and experience is also important, but only do so in controlled situations with other, more experienced kayakers present in support. If you don't push your boundaries you'll never progress, but do this in small increments, not big jumps.

A motto to remember is: **IF IN DOUBT, DON'T PUSH OUT.** If conditions deteriorate while you are on the water, get back ashore as soon as possible.

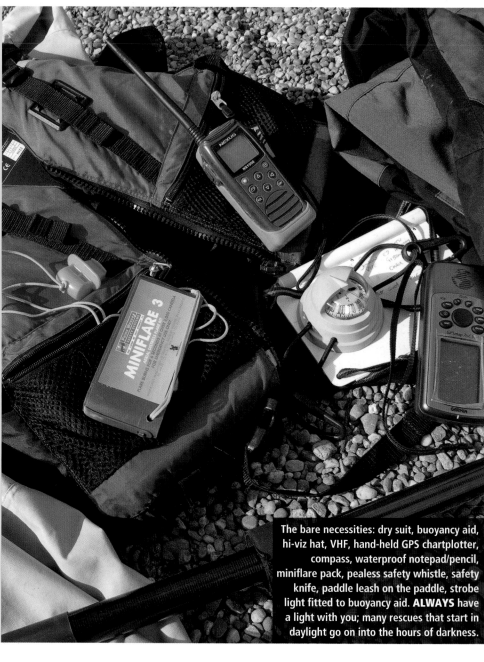

The bare necessities: dry suit, buoyancy aid, hi-viz hat, VHF, hand-held GPS chartplotter, compass, waterproof notepad/pencil, miniflare pack, pealess safety whistle, safety knife, paddle leash on the paddle, strobe light fitted to buoyancy aid. **ALWAYS** have a light with you; many rescues that start in daylight go on into the hours of darkness.

Kit List

The following is a kit list drawn up in conjunction with RNLI safety officers and is what they would like kayakers to carry as a minimum. It is not in order of importance. It is ALL of equal importance.

01 Buoyancy aid.

02 Pealess whistle attached to the buoyancy aid.

03 Hat – you lose the majority of your heat through the top of your head. In the sun, a hat can help prevent heatstroke. A wide-brimmed hat for the summer is a good idea and an insulated one for winter. If it's a high-viz one then that's even better.

04 Compass – checked for error (in other words, that it points in the right direction) – with no interference from other kit. A GPS can be carried in addition to a compass, not in place of it. A compass requires no power source to work – a GPS does and, therefore, can fail.

05 Chart of the area – a laminated photocopy is perfectly acceptable and legal for your own use.

06 VHF radio – 5W or above. Waterproofed with a fully charged battery and attached to the paddler, not the kayak.

07 Mobile phone in a waterproof case as backup to VHF, or as a minimum means of communication.

08 Paddle leash. Your paddle is your only means of propulsion – hang on to it.

09 Blunt-tipped rescue knife on your buoyancy aid, or where it is easily accessible. This is so you can cut yourself free from becoming entrapped in lines, anchor line or loose cordage.

10 Basic first-aid kit.

11 Suncream and lip salve.

12 Sunglasses.

13 Waterproof torch with fresh batteries. Many rescues start in daylight, but extend into the hours of darkness. A torch will help rescuers to locate you.

14 Drink and food.

15 Change of clothes in a dry bag.

16 Space blanket – can be carried in the first-aid kit. Be aware that a space blanket will NOT warm a cold person; it will actually keep a cold person cold, but will keep a warm person warm.

17 Towel – in with clothes in a dry bag.

18 Hypothermia bag.

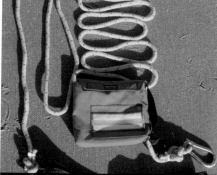

Rescue throw bag/towline. This is a simple mechanism to get a rope to an angler or for towing another boat.

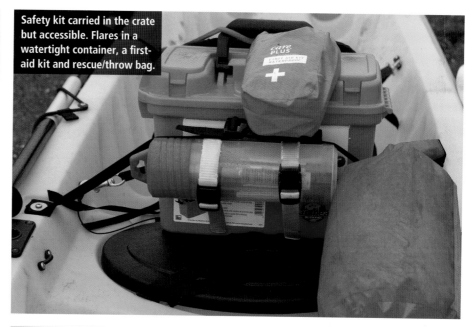

Safety kit carried in the crate but accessible. Flares in a watertight container, a first-aid kit and rescue/throw bag.

A dry suit with a rear, across-the-shoulders, zip. The rear zip doesn't impede paddling as much as a front, diagonal zip would.

You

The first part of safety lies with the paddler themselves. The physical and mental preparation of the paddler is as important as preparing your kayak and your kit. Ensure you are in good shape and are happy with the situation before you launch. RELAX – a paddler who is tense and unsure is more likely to get into a situation that they cannot control than one who is relaxed and already feels in control.

Know How To Use Your Kit Properly

Before you launch, find out the weather forecast for the day for the area you're in. Websites, Radio 4 and the coastguard are all ways of getting an accurate weather report. It's vitally important to monitor the tides and the sea state. Is the sea state going to change? Select your launch or make your decision accordingly. Be aware of

strong tidal influences that are likely to affect your ability to paddle to safety.

Be aware of alternative landing places; you don't have to return to where the car is parked in order to be safe. It might be inconvenient, but being ashore in the wrong place is safer than struggling to get back to your launch site in dangerous or difficult conditions.

Clothing

Paddling does leave you exposed to the elements and while you are active, keeping warm is relatively easy. However, once you sit still the cold can seep in very quickly. It's important to dress for the conditions prevailing. The air temperature and the water temperature must be taken into consideration, as well as mist, strong sun or driving rain. If you are uncomfortable you will be more liable to make mistakes, which could easily lead to a dangerous situation developing. Cold prevents your muscles from working as well as you might require them to.

Wet suits can be worn in mild conditions, but extra clothing on top might be required. Breathable dry suits are the best choice because they provide ease of movement, keep the wind out, allow perspiration to dissipate and provide a waterproof barrier. It must be remembered, though, that a dry suit provides no warmth or insulation whatsoever. Proper insulated and breathable underlayers must be worn with one.

In deciding what to wear, think of taking a dunking and prepare for it. If you go in the water without proper preparation, the cold water can leave an able-bodied person incapable of even righting their kayak and climbing back aboard. A good rule of thumb is: if the water is so cold that you couldn't swim in it comfortably for 30 minutes, then you need to dress for immersion.

Footwear

Make sure you choose comfortable over-shoes. Neoprene diver-type booties are a good choice. These have strong soles for use ashore and provide good feel for paddling. Buy a pair that allow you to wear good, insulated socks underneath without cutting off the circulation.

Gloves

Hands can suffer in the cold too. Paddling requires the use of your hands, so it makes sense to keep them warm. Paddling actually promotes circulation, so you may find that it is only when fishing that your hands get cold. Consider a pair of neoprene gloves that you can paddle in, and also put on to keep your fingers warmer when you're fishing. Paddle mits (pogies) are excellent for keeping your hands warm when paddling, but they can be a bit cumbersome when you put your paddle down.

And Finally... *Your Kayak*

Ensure your vessel is seaworthy. Check there are no leaks or damage and that everything is in place and working before you launch – have you put the hatch back on properly? CHECK that hatches are properly fastened.

You can use a dry bag (or two) to provide extra buoyancy within the hull by keeping air in it when you close it up. Alternatively, pool noodles or other closed-cell foam can be installed into the hull, as can car-tyre inner tubes, to provide positive buoyancy in case the hull is flooded.

REMEMBER: Experience is something that is gained immediately after the first time you need it.

This feature does not comprise a definitive list and it should be used in conjunction with any local knowledge you have of the area you are kayaking in. The list will provide some guidance, and no more, as to how to equip and prepare yourself for kayak fishing. The providers of this list do not accept any liability for omissions or inclusions. This is meant to be a guide and to help. Use your own judgement for any final decisions you may make.

An anchor can be used to set a position to fish or hold out in to have a rest.

A hand-held GPS, or a combined one with a fishfinder, will not only help to pinpoint your location but provide a 'trackback' route to get you home.

A fully equipped angler and kayak means a safer and more enjoyable time at sea.

The Domhoff Knot

Learn how to tie heavy monofilament to hooks, links and swivels to avoid losing a sharp-toothed monster.

When angling for fish such as sharks and congers it is important to use a biting trace that's thick enough to withstand the onslaught of their teeth. So anglers prefer to use wire traces, which are usually crimped.

With mono, however, crimping is not the best option as the line can slip through the crimp and it also weakens the line. The only other option is to tie a suitable knot and the Domhoff, also known as the Centauri, is ideal. Once learnt, it's easy to tie and has 97 per cent knot strength.

TopTips

1 Pull the knot tight against pliers or a T-bar. You're dealing with heavy gear and one slip can injure you – so be careful.

2 When tying very heavy line, two loops are all you'll need. But for lower-diameter lines, such as 30lb to 50lb, three loops will be needed.

3 Don't worry about this knot slipping, because the more you pull, the tighter it becomes.

How To Tie The Domhoff Knot

1 Pass the line through the hook or swivel and leave a tag of at least eight inches to work with.

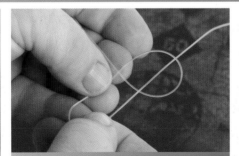

2 Form a loop around the running line and hold between thumb and forefinger.

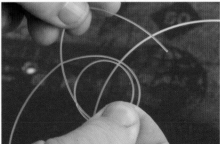

3 Form a second loop, the same as the first, and once again grip with your fingers to keep the loops open.

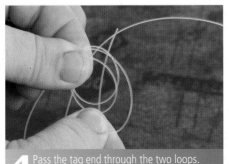

4 Pass the tag end through the two loops.

5 Tighten the coils a little, lubricate and slide the knot down, then pull tight using pliers or a T-bar.

6 Trim the waste and it's job done – a very strong and safe knot achieved with heavy mono!

TLD

ALL THE REEL YOU'LL EVER NEED

STRIKE • P UM LEVER DRAG. LESS 4 BALL BEARINGS

PRICES FROM
£109.99 SSP

Fashions come and go, but quality will always stand the test of time. Launched almost 25 years ago, the TLD's were a saltwater revelation, offering every angler the incredible precision, smoothness, power and accuracy that up 'til then had only been available in the worlds largest and most expensive reels. We've made a few adjustments over the years, 'tweaked' the drag, improved the bearings, but all in all it's much the same workhorse of a reel as it has always been. Solid, smooth, trustworthy and designed to give years of trouble-free service.

'The UK's favourite sea angling reel'

▶ Available in 15, 20 and 25 size models with prices starting from **£109.99 SSP**.
See the entire Shimano Boat range online at www.shimano.com, or in the 2011 Shimano Product Catalogue.

SHIMANO
2 YEAR
GUARANTEE

SHIMANO

Shore Plaice

Prepare to catch more **plaice** from the shore this coming season with our expert tips and advice.

Plaice are commonly confused with flounders due to them both having orangey-yellow spots evident on their backs, although on the plaice the spots are generally much more vivid. The best way to identify a plaice is to look for a series of four to seven boney knobs running backwards from between the eyes towards the pectoral fin.

The back of the plaice is typically light to medium brown with vivid orange spots. The belly is pearl-white, although occasionally it can be pockmarked with darker blotches.

Plaice spawn in the January to March period, usually in water over 30 metres deep. The eggs float in the surface layers, usually hatching between 10 and 20 days later. The larvae and post larvae live in the surface layers for another four to six weeks, at which time one eye migrates to the right-hand-side and, along with other body changes, the plaice becomes a flat, bottom-dwelling fish measuring roughly three-quarters of an inch long.

Female plaice become sexually mature at three to seven years and males at two to six years, and they can live for 30 years.

Their diet consists of brittle stars (a species of starfish), worms, crabs and shellfish such as razorfish and mussels; they are also adept at nipping the siphons off sand clams as they siphon nutrients from the water. They can also be formidable predators and will eat sandeels, and have occasionally been found with sprats and gobies inside their stomachs.

Tackle

Long-range fishing will give you your best chance of catching so choose a standard 4oz to 6oz beachcaster about 13 feet long, matched to a smaller ABU 6500-sized multiplier or Daiwa 7HT type filled with 15lb line, plus a 60lb shockleader. Alternatively, a longer European-style rod some 15 feet or more in length and a

How To Build A One-Hook Attractor Rig For Shore Plaice

1 Take 30 inches of 60lb rig-body line and tie on a Gemini lead link at one end.

2 Slide on a Breakaway Impact Shield followed by a 3mm rig bead and a crimp. Crimp this in place above the lead link, leaving about one-and-a-half inches for the Shield to slide in.

3 Slide on a rig crimp, a rig bead, a size 10 swivel, another bead and a crimp. Leave these loose for now. Finish the rig body with a size 4 rolling swivel.

4 The hook trace is a 24in length of 20lb line. Slide on alternate yellow and black beads, three of each, and tie on a size 2 Kamasan B940 Aberdeen hook.

5 Above the beads tie on a Powergum stop knot to prevent the beads from sliding up the hook trace during the cast.

6 Put the hook in the clip of the Bait Guard, slide the rig crimp below the hook-trace swivel up the rig-body line until the trace comes just tight, then crimp in place.

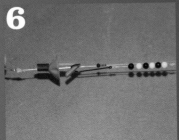

An ABU 6500 multiplier is a good reel choice for plaice fishing from the shore.

fixed-spool reel, again carrying 15lb line, will gain you more distance if your casting still needs a little work.

In estuaries a lighter bass rod of about 11ft 6in casting 2oz to 4oz is ample, matched to a smaller reel like an ABU 5500 C3 CT. In this situation, 12lb line is often enough, with a lighter 30lb leader, as the leads will be between 1oz and 3oz and long-range casting is not normally required.

When And Where

Plaice are found all around the UK and Irish coasts, as far south as the Mediterranean and to the north throughout Norway to Russia, all around Iceland and off the southern tip of Greenland.

As a general rule the UK season for plaice kicks off around the end of February in the south and west as far north as the Scottish borders, and a month later in the east and off the Scottish coast.

The early fish are thin but soon feed up and by late May are fat and healthy. They stay inshore until about October and then move out into deeper water.

Beach plaice are best fished for during the bigger spring tides as the fish are more active then and will feed more eagerly. Estuary plaice can be different and prefer to feed when the tides are smaller and less fierce.

In all areas the majority of plaice are caught during broad daylight, although occasionally the odd plaice is caught at night. They particularly like clear seas with minimum colour and good, general clarity.

They tend to concentrate over sand and shingle beds, but can also be found on mud mixed with sand. They also like seed-mussel beds at the mouths of estuaries and muddy channels where weed covered rocks form the estuary sides.

Two crab baits side by side on a wishbone rig.

Lugworms are a top plaice bait.

Bait

A top plaice bait is the body of a peeler crab cut in half and bound to the hook with elastic – you can add a long slice of squid to give the bait movement.

Other top baits for plaice are fresh blow and black lug, rag, fresh mussels, sand clams, razorfish and white rag if you can get it. They also take fresh sandeels and squid strips when fished on the drift with a plain bomb.

A single crab bait with attractors and beads.

4 TopTips For Plaice

1 Plaice like a moving bait so, where possible, change to a plain bomb or flat lead and let the tide pressure on the line sweep your bait slowly inshore in a wide, downtide arc. This tactic lets the bait fall into all those gutters and depressions and will locate the fish for you. If the tide run is minimal, try 'twitching' the bait back towards you a couple of inches at a time – this is often enough to induce a take.

2 Plaice feed best in very clear, calm seas. When this is the case, as with so much of this type of fishing, you'll catch more fish if you change your mono hook trace for a lighter, fluorocarbon hooklength. With plaice only normally caught up to 3lb or so, you can go as light as 10lb or 12lb to add more natural movement to the bait.

3 Plaice bites can be quite gentle. You'll see the rod tip rattle slightly a few times, but resist the urge to strike! Only when you see the rod tip pull properly over do you strike. When fishing in muddy water, plaice are more aggressive. They'll give a couple of small rattles and the tip will pull hard. When fishing a moving bait, the fish will be more aggressive as it chases the bait. When the fish hooks itself, the lead weight will stop drifting or slow right down and you'll see the rod tip pull over.

4 Always use fine-wired, but strong, size 1 or 2 Kamasan B940 Aberdeen-type hooks. Plaice have small mouths and these hooks are the best design suited to the way plaice feed. If you're missing bites and suspect they're from plaice, drop down to size 4 or even size 6 hooks. Always experiment with bead-colour combinations. White and green can be good over sand, as can blue and yellow when fishing close to mussel beds.

How To Use Sandeels

Learn how to use this most versatile bait with this easy-to-follow guide.

Sandeels are small eel-like fish that live in huge shoals along the western coast of Europe from the Baltic down to the Mediterranean.

They're a very important part of the food chain and support the largest fishery in the North Sea. They're also major targets for 'industrial fishing' for animal feed and fertilizer. Increasing fishing pressure is thought to be causing problems for some of their natural predators, including many species of fish and sea birds such as puffins, terns and kittiwakes.

Of the five species of sandeel in the North Sea, two species of interest to us are the lesser and greater sandeel; the latter is also called launce.

If you live near the coast there are several ways to collect sandeels – by seine net, jigging feathers with very small hooks while drifting over sandbanks, or raking or forking through coarse sand at low tide. Sandeels are quite delicate and can be difficult to keep but they can be kept alive for a few hours under sacking soaked in sea water. One of the best methods of keeping them alive is to use a purpose-built livebait bucket with an aerator; this should sustain them for several hours but they must be kept cool and out of the sun.

If you're unable to collect live eels, most tackle shops stock packs of frozen sandeels and many anglers actually prefer to use these rather than fresh eels.

Fresh or frozen, they're superb bait for most species of fish – both pelagic (inhabitants of the upper layers) and bottom feeders – and can be used whole, in fillets or in tiny strips to tip off worm baits.

Live sandeels drift fished along the sea bed or freelined are deadly bait for bass, pollack, tope, turbot and brill, while float-fished small sandeels catch mackerel, garfish and scad. Small sections or tiny fillets tipping off worm are good for whiting, bream, gurnard and many other species.

The traditional bait bucket has an aerator clipped on the side.

How To Bait Up With Sandeels

1 Frozen sandeels make excellent bait for many species.

2 When using a live sandeel, simply pass the hook through its lips.

3 Worm baits can be tipped off with a piece of sandeel fillet.

4 To use a whole sandeel, trim off the head and tail to let the juices out.

5 Insert the hook through the tail end and thread it on the hook in the same way you would with a worm.

6 Bring the hook point out two-thirds of the way down the body then pass the hook through the head to lock it in position.

The Rapala Knot

Learn how to join line to your lures so that they can work properly when fished.

When fishing with a lure it's essential that it can move in the water as naturally as possible. The best way to make this happen is by attaching it to your line via a loop so that it can move freely.

If you were to simply tie it direct, every movement of the lure would be absorbed, to an extent, by the running line – therefore restricting its movement.

The best, and most secure, knot to create this effect is the Rapala. Follow our step-by-step guide to help increase your catch rate by improving your lure presentation to the fish.

TopTips

1 Use saliva to lubricate the knot when tightening.

2 Be careful not to nick the lines when trimming up.

3 Take every care not to become impaled on a hook while you're tying the knot.

How To Tie The Rapala Knot

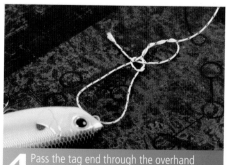

1 Form an overhand loop, allowing six inches or so for the tag.

2 Pass the tag through the eye of the lure and back through the overhand knot.

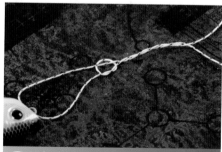

3 Make three turns down the running line.

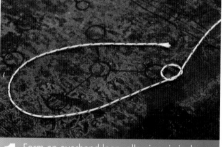

4 Pass the tag end through the overhand knot.

5 Now thread the tag end through the loop you just formed.

6 Lubricate with saliva, pull it all tight and trim the tag.

European Three-Hook
Sweeper
RIG

History Of The Rig

The European three-hook sweeper rig first saw action about eight years ago, initially being used very successfully by Dutch competition anglers in conjunction with 15ft to 18ft rods. With the introduction of these rods over in the UK, the rig was also adopted by UK match anglers when targeting fish in generally calm, clear or cold seas in daylight… and proved highly successful.

These longer rods allow a much longer trace body to be used, so you can cover a wider area of the sea bed, plus you can dramatically alter the way the bait is presented at different lengths along the rig compared with a standard three-hook rig. This can make a huge difference to the overall catch rate, especially in difficult conditions.

It's called a sweeper rig because it uses a long trace at the base of it that can wash freely around with the tide, but still keeps the bait tight to the sea bed. In addition there are two hooks higher up the rig, giving a more standard type of presentation, making the rig highly versatile.

How It Works

This rig works well at both close and medium range fished with a grip lead. The long, lower hooklength will wash over the sea bed in a sweeping fashion, which is where the rig's name comes from. Ideally you need a little lateral tide run to achieve the best from this rig, as this will spin the blade and make the bait lift occasionally to add attraction. Adding floating beads can aid this – but keep these to just enough to occasionally lift the bait, not fully suspend it.

Used with a plain lead you can cover a huge area of sea bed and pick individual fish that otherwise would be missed. However, you will need some tide run and you must fish to a tight line between the weight and rod tip, because if there is little or no tide, the lower trace can tangle.

Up And Down...

You can change the presentation of the top two hooks at close range by simply raising the angle of the rod tip a little in your rod rest. With the tip at a very low angle, the top two hooklengths will fish baits tight to the sea bed. Lift the height of the rod tip fractionally and you can have the middle hook still on the sea bed and the top hook fishing up above it. Add more rod-tip height and you can have the top two hook baits fishing just up off the sea bed to target free-swimming round fish.

Another good tip when fishing as above is to occasionally tighten the line to the rod tip, leave it for a few seconds, then release two or three feet of line to create a downward bow. This effectively lifts and drops the bait, adding natural movement that inquisitive fish will move in towards.

Go Light For A Bite!

In very clear seas and bright daylight you can remove the attractor beads and spoon, and replace the hooklengths with lighter 8lb fluorocarbon. Also, drop the size of the hooks down to size 6 or smaller Aberdeen or

Build Sequence

1 Start with 7ft 6in of 60lb clear mono line and at one end tie on a Gemini rig clip.

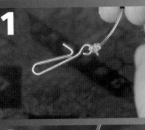

2 Add a rig crimp, a size 3mm rig bead, a size 10 swivel, another rig bead and a crimp. Crimp these in place one inch above the rig clip.

3 Slide on an inverted Paul Kerry or Breakaway bait clip and let it slide freely, which allows for easy adjustment and also avoids the snood stretching through casting pressure.

4 Slide on another crimp, a rig bead, a size 10 swivel, a rig bead and a crimp, followed by another crimp bead and swivel assembly.

5 Finish the main rig body by tying on a size 4 swivel to act as the main rig-to-leader connector.

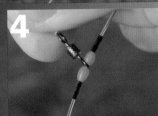

6 The lower hooklength is 20lb line and can be 45 to 90 inches long. Slide on a rubber rig stop, followed by a pearl-coloured bead, a small silver plastic flasher spoon and two more pearl beads. The hook size for general fishing is a size 2 Kamasan B940 Aberdeen.

7 Crimp the middle hook snood in place 60 inches above the rig clip, and the top swivel is positioned tight underneath the rig-connector swivel.

8 Use 20lb line for the two top hooklengths, which should be 10 inches long, and should have a red, a yellow and another red bead and a size 2 B940 Kamasan Aberdeen hook.

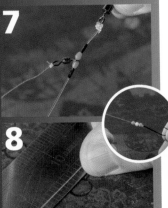

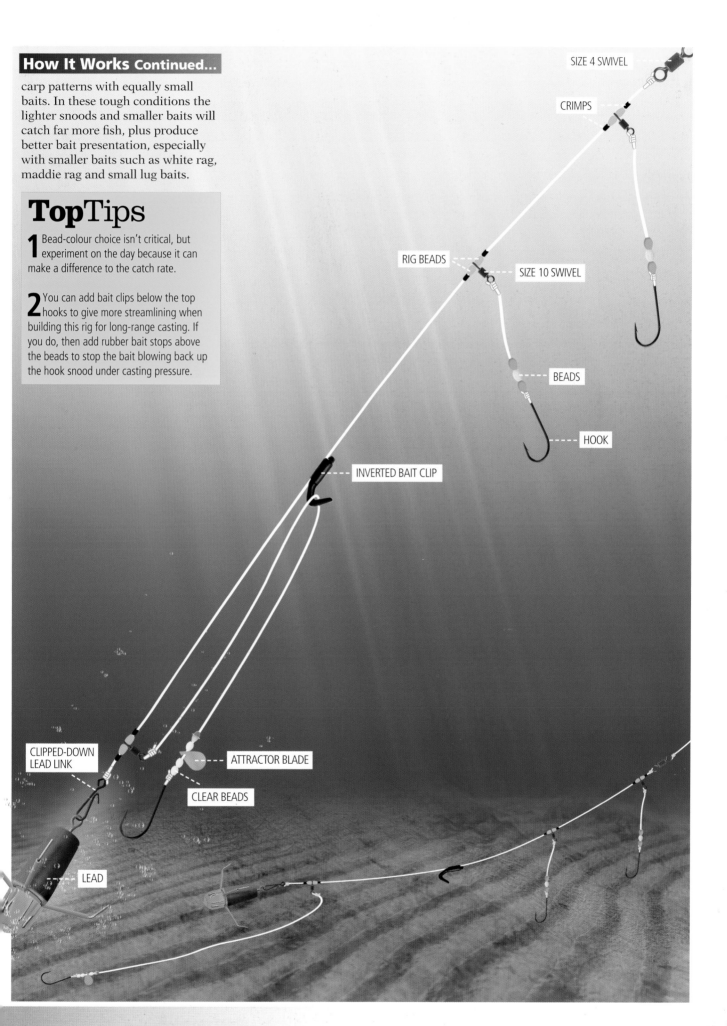

How It Works Continued...

carp patterns with equally small baits. In these tough conditions the lighter snoods and smaller baits will catch far more fish, plus produce better bait presentation, especially with smaller baits such as white rag, maddie rag and small lug baits.

TopTips

1 Bead-colour choice isn't critical, but experiment on the day because it can make a difference to the catch rate.

2 You can add bait clips below the top hooks to give more streamlining when building this rig for long-range casting. If you do, then add rubber bait stops above the beads to stop the bait blowing back up the hook snood under casting pressure.

SIZE 4 SWIVEL

CRIMPS

RIG BEADS

SIZE 10 SWIVEL

BEADS

HOOK

INVERTED BAIT CLIP

CLIPPED-DOWN LEAD LINK

ATTRACTOR BLADE

CLEAR BEADS

LEAD

IT SEEMS THERE'S NO LONGER A SLOT FOR ANGLERS.

Fishing from a pier or a dock around England is getting harder.

Local councils are giving over these historic and ecologically important sites to luxury developments, amusement arcades and fun fairs and banning anglers from many traditional marks.

Health and safety regulations and prohibitive parking laws are putting a further squeeze on the humble rod and line angler. With the result that the most traditional of seaside attractions is in decline.

That's why the angling community needs the Angling Trust.

We're here to represent **all** angling; sea, coarse and game anglers alike. And help them fight the decisions and polices that threaten their right to enjoy their sport.

Join us and you'll be joining a powerful voice for the future of angling in England.
Visit **www.anglingtrust.net** to learn more or call **0844 770 0616** today.

IF YOU WON'T HELP PROTECT OUR WATERS... WHO WILL?

ANGLING TRUST

THE VOICE OF ANGLING

Shore Mullet

Learn how to bag up with **mullet** this season with our top tips and tricks.

Mullet are sporting and great fun to target!

Identification of the three true mullet species is not easy unless you have a practised eye. The body shapes of all three mullet are similar; it's the lips and eyes that give each one away.

The thick-lipped mullet has a broad upper lip – its depth being more than half the diameter of its eye. The thin-lipped sports a thinner upper lip that's less than half the depth of the eye diameter, and its pectoral fin, if folded forward, does not reach the eye. The golden grey also has a thin upper lip – its depth again less than half the eye diameter – but if the pectoral fin is folded forward it covers the rear edge of the eye.

The coloration of the thick-lipped mullet is dark grey, sometimes greeny grey, with six or seven grey bands running lengthways along the flanks, and with a white belly. The thin-lipped is more grey-blue on the back and is silvery on the sides, with faint grey lines running the length of the flanks, often with a dark spot at the base of the pectoral fin. The golden grey mullet is grey-blue on the back with silver sides, and grey stripes running lengthways along the flanks. It also sports a conspicuous golden spot on the cheek and gill cover, although all mullet types sometimes look slightly golden on the gill cover.

Thick-lipped and golden grey mullet are found all around the UK and Ireland and as far north as southern Norway and the southeast corner of Iceland, then right down to the European coast, throughout the Mediterranean and into north Africa. Thin-lipped mullet are most common in the southern half of the UK and Ireland, venturing north as far as the southern tip of Norway and southwards, taking in the Mediterranean.

Mullet feed by sifting mud, extracting worms, small crustaceans and plant matter, but bigger mullet also feed on small fish and even crustaceans.

Mullet are migratory, showing first in the south of the UK

Build A Mullet Bubble Float Rig

A simple but highly effective float rig for mullet uses a bubble float, which can be cast to greater distances than traditional float tackle and is perfect for working surface-floating baits.

1 The best bubble floats are clear, cylindrical Okuma or Bonnand ones that are instantly adjustable. You can add water to the float to increase casting weight.

2 Remove the plastic plug, then slide the reel line or fluorocarbon through the slot in the top of the plug. Pass the line down through the centre of the float, pulling about 18 inches of line through, then replace the plug in the float.

3 To the end of the reel line below the float, tie on a size 10 rolling swivel. To the end of the swivel add about five feet of 6lb to 8lb fluorocarbon line.

4 Finish with a size 10 Kamasan B980 Specimen Eyed hook.

You're not using the float for visual indication; it's there to give casting weight and to suspend the line on the water's surface, allowing you to let surface-floating bread wash down with the tide to feeding fish. This is where you'll watch the bread bait, looking for it to disappear in a swirl as a mullet takes it off the surface.

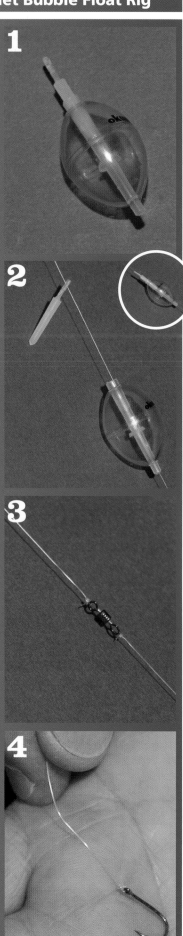

A golden grey has a distinct golden spot on the gill cover.

Thick lips are so called due to the broad upper part of the mouth.

mainland and Ireland in April and working further north through May and June. The fish typically leave in October with the first frosts, although it can be later in the south. Golden grey mullet are often the last mullet to arrive, showing in May and June, and they leave earlier in September, especially at the northern extreme of their range.

Little scientific work has been done on mullet, but it's thought that they don't breed in UK waters, with breeding taking place to the south.

When And Where To Fish

All mullet favour harbours and marinas, but the thick-lipped, and especially the thin-lipped, will travel right up to the freshwater-divide line in estuaries and can often be seen swimming inside estuary drainage creeks, across mud flats and in the mouths of small bays that are well inland. Thick-lipped mullet also work open beaches, especially in late July and August when weed maggots are available.

Golden grey mullet differ by also working open surf beaches tight in among the surf tables, deeper marinas and will also frequent open rock marks that drop onto clean sand.

Thick-lipped and thin-lipped mullet are cautious and shy fish so, at times, are best fished for when boat traffic is low and visitors are few, such as at dawn and towards dusk in estuaries, but in harbours they get used to people and can be fished for at any time. They tend to come in with the new flood tide and stay until about an hour after.

Golden grey mullet working open beaches show with the flood tide and will work the beach until high water, often disappearing on the ebb. Again, this is common but not certain.

Shore Mullet Tackle

Every mullet angler will have his own preference, but a good all-round choice for open water, harbours and marinas is a light Avon-type rod that's about 12 feet in length. This has the backbone to turn fish away from pontoons and structure if needs be.

Match this to a 3000 or 4000-sized fixed-spool reel, such as a Penn Sargus or Shimano or

Daiwa equivalent. Line, again, is a personal thing – some anglers prefer mono between 4lb and 6lb breaking strain. Others prefer 12lb to 15lb braid, but use a 15ft section of 8lb fluorocarbon.

Clear loaded waggler floats are most commonly used with a little shot, added to set the float just in the surface film, but clear bubble floats are also highly effective, especially when trotting bread baits down to surface-feeding fish. Hook sizes need to be from a size 6 down to 12. A size 8 or 10 is a good common size for bread baits.

Baits For Mullet

Bread is by far the best bait. A cheap white sliced loaf is perfect for thick-lipped mullet as it is doughy and can be moulded around the hook to leave the hook point just clear. Use a piece

about the size of a 10p coin, although mullet will often take much bigger bits when feeding hard. Thick-lipped mullet will also take small bits of mackerel flesh without the skin in harbours where boats get cleaned down. They learn to eat other man-made foods that wash into harbours and creeks, such as bits of pasta, sausage meat, corn, small pieces of cooked shrimps and will often take small bits of ragworm and lugworm fished in front of floats.

Thin-lipped mullet can be caught using small Mepps spinners with a single size 8 hook attached and baited with a single harbour ragworm (maddie). Recent success has also been achieved using the smaller 4in Berkley Gulp! Sandworms – which are lifelike when moved – in the Bloody colour.

When targeting golden grey

mullet in the surf, use a small, drilled bullet that's stopped by a small bead and swivel and use a 36in length of 8lb fluorocarbon to a size 6 long-shank hook. Bait this with a small bunch of maddies and allow the lead to be washed in along the surf tables while keeping a tight line to feel for plucking bites. Often you'll see the fish swimming through the shallow surf right in front of you in small shoals and just a few yards out. Casts of just 20 yards are often enough.

A good mullet groundbait is just mashed-up bread with some thinly shredded mackerel flesh and a little pilchard oil. A good method is to suspend a small mesh bag of the mash in the tide, letting it just touch the water's surface to trickle scent and bits of food and draw the fish to you.

5 TopTips For Mullet

1 When groundbaiting for mullet in harbours, creeks and on mud flats, do this at the same tide stage every day, not at the same time of day. Mullet will associate a particular state of tide in that place with food and, once used to feeding there, will return day after day and become catchable. When it comes to fishing, only groundbait lightly to keep the fish occupied and not fully fed.

2 Mullet are intelligent and learn when food will be available. This especially applies to waste pipes that run into harbours. Mullet will collect here just before the pipe is scheduled to flow and will feed on domestic food waste that washes down. These are excellent places to fish. Also, fish in lagoons where people feed swans with bread because the mullet will learn to take bread freely off the surface in these conditions.

3 When fishing a creek, estuary or harbour wall with no cover, keep a low profile. Mullet are shy fish and even a shadow from a moving rod will scare them off. Try to blend in with the background by wearing dull clothes, keep below the skyline and keep movement and noise to an absolute minimum.

4 Mullet can be caught by legering. Use a two-hook paternoster with 12in hook snoods of 8lb fluorocarbon. Gently lower this to the sea bed using a light lead weight to fish above bread groundbait. This works especially well in harbours and marinas.

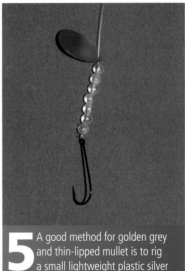

5 A good method for golden grey and thin-lipped mullet is to rig a small lightweight plastic silver spoon above a series of small pearl beads with a size 8 hook, baiting with maddies. This is highly effective in harbours, river mouths and from the open beach when fishing the surf using a simple slow retrieve.

New, Complete
Imax
Clothing Range

Something you cannot be without when fishing is decent clothing. You are up against the elements and, especially in winter, you will need some serious protection.

For years, Imax has provided the serious sea fisherman with durable and thought-through clothing, which has set new standards for safety at sea and raised the bar in terms of comfort and functionality. It has fast become the preferred brand for Nordic sea angling guides and, now, Imax is ready with a whole new line-up of sea equipment,

which will excite all the serious sea anglers out there. It's the most complete programme ever developed by Imax, and the design and production period has been one of extreme dedication, vision and attention to detail.

The range includes the Nautic and Aquanaut flotation suits, the Sea Ranger and Storm Ply Lux dry suits, the Thermo suit, a fleece undersuit, as well as a life

vest, boat boots, and the two sets of gloves – the Oceanic and the Baltic. The whole range comes in a very stylish bright red, black and white colour combination, and all together it covers every imaginable need in terms of sea fishing – no matter the weather and time of year. It's perfect for sea fishing in the in the UK, northern areas of Europe, the Baltic region and in Scandinavia.

SEA RANGER DRY SUIT

STORM PLY LUX DRY SUIT

AQUANAUT FLOTATION SUIT

FLEECE SUIT

Designed For Anglers...

The Nautic and Aquanaut flotation suits conform to both CE and international ISO 12402-5 standards, are incredibly lightweight and incorporate plenty of details specifically for the sea angler – for instance: special sleeves and cuffs; large, zipped, handwarmer pockets and elasticated, neoprene shoulders. Other details include: abrasion guard; reinforced knees, seat, elbows and shoulders; highly breathable, low-density buoyancy foam; safety whistles; three-way, ergonomically engineered, adjustable hoods and more. They're both two-piece models, are available at two different price levels and have real competitive edges.

Breathable

The Sea Ranger and Storm Ply Lux dry suits are one-piece, breathable and waterproof specialised for fishing. They're made from a robust, tear-resistant shell fabric but with a very high breathability, which essentially means that, despite the fact that they're 100 per cent waterproof, they will allow the body to breathe. When it comes to sea fishing in cold and treacherous waters, these dry suits are perfect. They're surprisingly comfortable and will keep the angler warm and dry. The suits incorporate heavy-duty, waterproof YKK zips across the shoulders; neoprene glideskin seals at the neck and wrist; strong, integrated neoprene socks; heat-seal taped seams and much more. The Sea Ranger and Storm Ply Lux suits are perfect in combination with the new Imax life vest – which is a 150N, CE and EN-approved automatic inflation vest.

A Thermo suit has also been developed for the new Imax range, and it's perfect in combination with the new fleece undersuit – which is also great for wearing underneath the other suits as well. The Thermo suit is an extremely warm and 100 per cent waterproof, two-piece garment made from heavy nylon shell fabric, and comes fitted with a detachable hood, big outer pockets, velcro cuffs and reinforced buckles. The fleece suit is one-piece with elastic at the waist, Lycra socks for a better fit and a full, two-way zip for easy access.

Besides the suits and the life vest, the new Imax clothing range also includes new, neoprene, special-grip boat boots for use with the dry suits, as well as new, 100 per cent waterproof and breathable gloves (the Baltic and Oceanic), which are made from the finest and most comfortable Spandex, neoprene, polyurethane and synthetic-leather materials.

With this new range, Imax has once again set new standards for functional oceanic clothing.

For more information, please contact **Svendsen Sport** at *info@ svendsen-sport. com* or by phone on: 01827 59659

OCEANIC GLOVES

BOAT BOOTS

BALTIC GLOVES

NAUTIC FLOTATION SUIT TROUSERS

NAUTIC FLOTATION SUIT JACKET

THERMO SUIT JACKET

LIFE VEST

Boat Tope

Learn how to improve your **tope** catch rate from the boat with our top tips and tricks!

The tope is a true sportfish and a shark that will test you on light tackle.

The tope is relatively easy to identify. It can only really be confused with the smoothhound. The quick way to check between the two is the teeth – the tope has true shark's teeth: triangulated, serrated and sharply pointed, perfect for grabbing and cutting live prey. The smoothhound has flat, blunt teeth used for grinding crabs and shellfish.

Another identifiable area is the pectoral fin. On the tope the pectoral fin is long, but on the smoothhound it is short and more triangulated. Also, if you look at the lower tail lobe of the tope, this again is longer and comes to a point, whereas on the smoothhound the lower tail lobe is just short and rounded.

The tope is typically a shallow-water fish found in depths down to 100 feet, but can occasionally go as deep as 600 feet.

The tope's coloration is typically uniform grey with a white belly, but when living on sand the back will take on a fawny-brown colour.

The breeding season is typically from mid-April to mid-July and takes place over sandbanks. Females give birth to live young some 15 inches in length. Litters of 20 to 40 pups are common, but larger females can produce more. The pups are born in late summer, usually close to shore, and adjacent to reef structures. It's no coincidence that this birthing period coincides with the smaller pack tope migrating offshore, saving the small pups from being eaten by their own kind.

The tope's diet consists of

Build A Boat Tope Rig

The most popular tope rig is a simple sliding leger using 150lb mono.

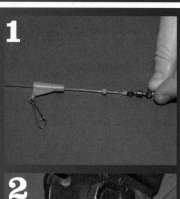

1 Using a 60lb/80lb shockleader, slide onto this a zip slider and a 5mm bead. To the end of the leader tie on a size 2 rolling swivel.

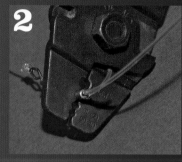

2 To the free eye of the size 2 swivel, crimp on 46 inches of 150lb mono.

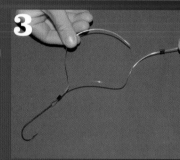

3 Take the free end of the heavy mono and slide on two crimps and a Mustad Viking 79515 hook size 6/0. Now pass the free end of 150lb line through the crimp nearest the hook ready for securing.

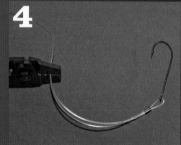

4 Pass the free end of line through the top crimp to form a loop in the line about eight inches long and crimp in place to secure the loop.

5 Now crimp the bottom crimp in place above the hook, but leave the hook enough room to move freely around in for natural bait presentation.

6 You now have a double section of line that combats the teeth of the tope. Trim off any excess tag end and it's job done.

---

mainly bottom-dwelling fish such as dabs, flounders, whiting, poor cod, pouting, small codling and gurnards, but on reef ground small black bream and bass are the main targets. Contrary to popular belief, mackerel do not form a major part of the tope's diet. A fit mackerel can leave a fit tope way behind in a race. Tope can usually only catch injured or weak mackerel.

When And Where To Fish

Tope are found all round the UK and Ireland, although numbers are limited north of the Yorkshire coast up the Scottish east coast as far as the east side of Orkney. They are also found as far north as the southern coast of Norway, throughout the Mediterranean and down the north African coast.

Some of the best fishing is in the Wash off the Lincolnshire coast, in the Thames Estuary, off Swansea and Tenby in South Wales, Cardigan Bay in mid Wales, off Blackpool and inside the Solway Firth. Ireland's best tope fishing is off the east coast between Bray and Kilmore Quay, in the Shannon Estuary, and in the north in Lough Swilly. Big tope also come from Strangford and Carlingford Loughs in Northern Ireland.

The season for tope begins in late March with fish showing from the Welsh coast and the Thames Estuary. By May they have moved north as far as the Wash and the Lancashire coast. By June they have crossed the water border into Scotland and can be caught in July and August as far north as the Orkney Islands. Tope can be caught late in November, but in southern areas they move offshore in late

July, leaving smaller pack tope that stay until August or so. Big fish linger later off the Cornish and Welsh coasts with odd fish showing in deeper water between November and February in mild winters.

Small tope up to 30lb or so work in packs and are wide ranging, depleting the food supply in one area and moving on to the next. Bigger fish over 40lb will most likely be females and are often found swimming alone, although in the period May to June they can be found with the smaller male tope when breeding.

Boat Tackle

The days of 50lb-class rods are long gone for tope fishing. Anglers should now look at light 12lb/15lb-class rods matched to smaller lightweight reels, such as the Penn Fathom 20s, ABU Alphamar 16s and Shimano Toriums loaded with 15lb/18lb mono when fishing shallow water. In deeper water a 20lb-class rod and the same reels loaded with 20lb mono may be the better choice. Braid line is also good, but not as popular when fishing for big, fast-running fish like tope, although in fast tidal areas it may be the only option to fish. If you choose braid, tie on a clear mono leader at least twice the length of the rod to provide some elasticity when a fish is close to the boat.

In areas of fast tides and shallow water, such as the Thames Estuary, casting away from the boat is very effective because it puts the baits out of the scare area created by the tide flowing past the hull. Most anglers choose a 9ft 6in to 10ft rod rated to cast 4oz to 10oz, coupled with reels such as the Penn 515 and 525 Mag 2s, Abu

Tope have sharp teeth, whereas smoothhounds have grinding pads.

7000 series and Daiwa Sloshs popularly loaded with 15lb to 20lb main line. Although, again, some anglers choose braid for this because casting range is relatively short – under 50 yards – and the thin diameter of the braid allows lighter leads to hold efficiently.

When targeting tope at the edges of very shallow reefs, you can also use fixed-spool reels. Those chosen are usually Baitrunner types with the Penn 560 Live Liner and Shimano Baitrunner reels top contenders. These allow you to cast with minimal or no lead weight to give natural presentation, especially during slack-water periods. Having the Baitrunner option to give line freely, but allowing you to re-engage the reel by a simple turn of the handle, is ideal for this style of fishing.

Tope Baits

Most anglers assume that mackerel, usually as a tail or head flapper with the backbone cut out, is the best bait – and it does work – but there are more consistent baits. The best bait is half a small dab cut diagonally across the body and using the head and guts as the bait. Tope feed on dabs primarily and this is why it's the top bait. Alternatively, use half a whiting, head half again, whole small poor cod, pouting and even small pollack, all of which can often outfish mackerel.

If you're using cut fish baits, then half a small mackerel, half a bluey or a squid all make good

A whole poor cod will often outfish mackerel baits.

alternative baits.

Most anglers make the mistake of using baits that are far too big. Although a shark species, the tope has a relatively small mouth and will pick up baits then drop them repeatedly if they're too big. Baits of no more than six inches long are ample.

5 TopTips For Tope

1 There is a difference of opinion over tope-trace construction. Some anglers prefer to use heavy 150lb mono as described in the boat tope rig, as they feel it's friendlier to the fish. Others choose to use a short section of 50lb wire. The facts are that in deep water a tope will pick up the heavy mono without problem, especially in a tide that unrolls the coils of stiff mono. It's a different matter when fishing close to shallow reefs in gin-clear water just eight feet deep with no tide run, though. In these circumstances a tope will either shy away from the mono, or pick up and instantly drop the bait. This is when wire is the better option.

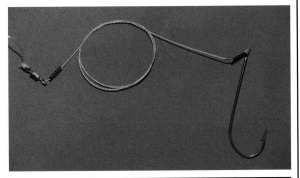

4 When fishing over reef ground in clear, shallow water and choosing to fish with heavy mono hook traces, use a permanent black marker to colour the line. This will then camouflage itself among the rocks and stop the tope from being spooked.

2 If a tope picks up and drops the bait, leave it there. The odds are that another tope is close behind and will take the same bait. Alternatively, if the bait is dropped, twitch the bait forwards by retrieving a few feet of line to make the tope think an injured fish is trying to get away. This will result in an instant strike.

3 Too many anglers' hook sizes are far too big for tope and they will miss fish as a consequence. Typically, a strong Viking pattern size 6/0 is ample and is more than strong enough to land record fish. For bigger baits, go no bigger than a Mustad Barbless Tope and Ray hook size 8/0. Alternatively you can crimp the barb on a hook down with pliers. Having barbless hooks will not cost you any lost fish providing you keep the line tight at all times.

5 When tope fishing, always set the reel in free spool with the ratchet alarm engaged. This allows the tope to run off with the bait, but feel minimal resistance. Also set the drag to give line under steady pressure well below the line's breaking strain. Don't strike the fish with the rod. Let the fish run a few yards of line off the reel then put the reel in gear, and let the drag set the hook against the weight of the fish as the line comes tight.

The Shark RIG

History Of The Rig

Although sharks were targeted on rod and line before World War II, it was bored former fighter and bomber pilots in the post-war period who brought sportfishing for sharks into the limelight by starting up charter-boat fishing off the southwest coast.

These guys fished heavy – the first traces were made from car brake cable in a single length with heavy crimps of copper tubing, flattened with cold chisels. Their hooks were size 12/0 and 14/0, but times have moved on and current traces are far more advanced.

The shark trace described here is similar to most shark traces, but is the pattern rig expert Mike Thrussell has come to trust over 30 years of targeting sharks in the UK and all over the world. This is a typical blue shark trace, but the basic pattern is the same for porbeagles – just use a heavier 400lb biting trace at the end or 400lb wire all through.

How It Works

The total length of the two unattached wire sections is 15 feet, but with the crimps and loops added and fixed you will end up with a 14ft 3in trace.

You need this length to combat the shark's abrasive skin, as the body and tail can come into contact with the trace, which has to take massive abuse.

A top-quality big-game ball-bearing link swivel is best to attach the trace to the reel line, clipping the link inside the top doubled-wire loop, so it can be changed quickly if required.

The middle swivel needs to be top quality and able to rotate under the pressure of a shark's rolling, spinning and corkscrewing when hooked, which will cause kinks in wire traces without swivels. It must also take some of the shark's weight when it's held at the side of the boat prior to either release in the water or being manually lifted onto the deck for tagging, photography and release.

This big swivel also gives the boat's 'wire man' something big to hold for a better grip.

The trace is split in two with the main long length of trace being the rubbing leader, and the trace below the second swivel the biting piece. This means you can replace the biting piece at any time without destroying the main trace, which helps keeps costs down because wire is expensive in long lengths. To make a heavier trace for porbeagle sharks, use 400lb wire for both sections.

TopTips

1 When you've cut the wire, put a spot of superglue onto the tag ends. This will seal the wires and prevent them from splitting up when you're pushing them through a tight crimp tube.

2 Make a few traces with the top rubbing leader made from heavy and clear 400lb commercial mono. In calmer seas even blue sharks will see the full length of the leader and bite wire and shy off or remain spooked. If you switch to the heavy-mono rubbing leader they'll take the bait with more confidence, even though they can still see the bite wire. The mono is crimped in the same way as the wire.

Build Sequence

1 Take 11ft 6in of 49-strand 200lb wire.

2 Slide on a double crimp with a tube diameter big enough to take the diameter of the wire you're using.

3 Pass the end of the wire over the top of itself to form a loop. Pass the tag end of wire through the loop three times so that the tag end faces back towards the crimp. This is called a Flemish loop.

4 Pull down on top of the wire loop to tighten it, then pass the tag end through the free tube of the crimp. Ideally the tag end should pass nearly all the way through the crimp – but not quite. You may need to recut the tag end to size to achieve this. This stops sharp edges catching your fingers when handling the trace.

5 Using proper crimping pliers, place the crimp in the plier's jaws with the tubes positioned one above the other, so that they look like a figure of eight. Close the crimp securely, making sure the crimp is evenly closed along its length.

6 To the free end of the wire, crimp on a size 5/0 swivel using the Flemish loop.

7 To the free end of the swivel attach 3ft 6in of 200lb wire using the Flemish loop and crimp.

8 To the end of the wire, and using the Flemish loop, crimp on a size 6/0 or 8/0 Mustad O'Shaughnessy 3406 hook. This completes the trace.

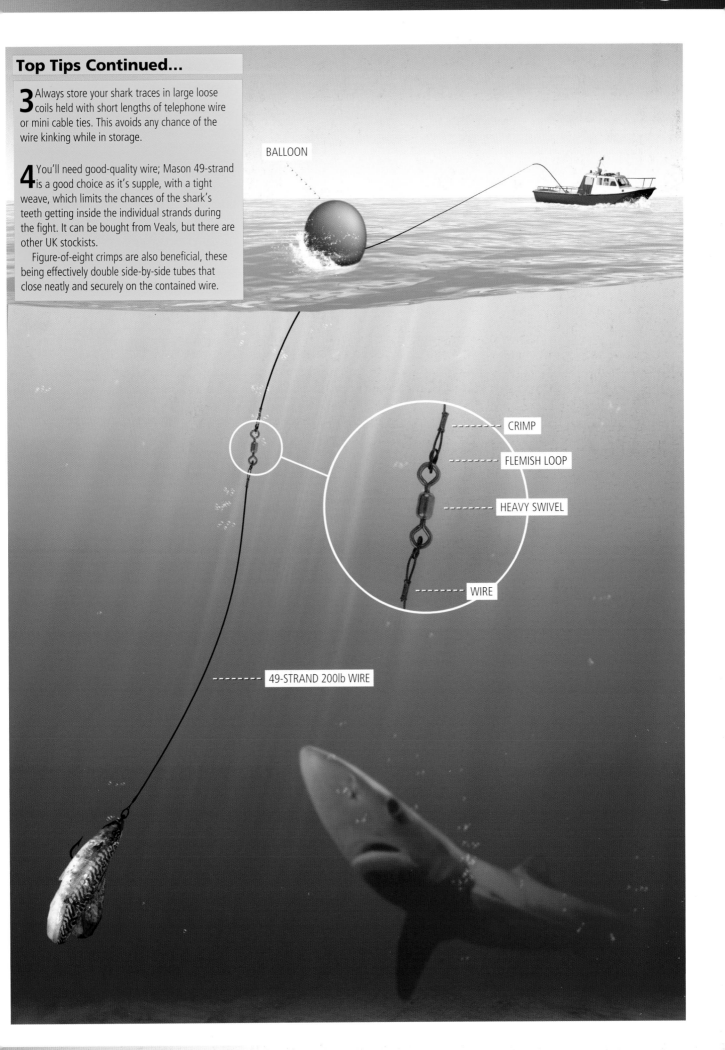

Top Tips Continued...

3 Always store your shark traces in large loose coils held with short lengths of telephone wire or mini cable ties. This avoids any chance of the wire kinking while in storage.

4 You'll need good-quality wire; Mason 49-strand is a good choice as it's supple, with a tight weave, which limits the chances of the shark's teeth getting inside the individual strands during the fight. It can be bought from Veals, but there are other UK stockists.

Figure-of-eight crimps are also beneficial, these being effectively double side-by-side tubes that close neatly and securely on the contained wire.

BALLOON

CRIMP

FLEMISH LOOP

HEAVY SWIVEL

WIRE

49-STRAND 200lb WIRE

Which Boat Rod?

Save time, money and avoid confusion when choosing your boat rod with this simple advice.

With so many to choose from, selecting the correct boat rod can be a difficult task. The best way is to pick one that is best suited to the kind of fishing that you do most.

For general boat fishing, where you're dropping over the side onto clean or mixed ground, something in the 15lb to 20lb class will be fine for most species, or even as light as 12lb if you're targeting bream and flatties. If you fish over reefs and rough ground for congers and bull huss in, say, 100 feet of water, you'll need to look at something in the 30lb-class range to cope with the stronger currents and bigger fish. If you prefer offshore fishing for sharks or go wrecking in 200 feet of water for huge congers, then you'll need more powerful gear, such as a 50lb-class outfit, to cope with strong fish and currents.

If most of your marks are inshore over clean ground then a 9ft to 10ft uptider will enable you to cast rigs well away from the noise of the boat.

No rod will do everything, but there are those available that have two or three different tips that fit into one butt. For example, the Fox Multi Boat Tri-Tip has 10lb, 20lb and 30lb tips, allowing you to select the best one for the species that you're after or the type of ground that you're fishing over. Overall, choose a rod with a supple tip rather than one that's as stiff as a poker because a bending rod will tire the fish more quickly and avoid you tearing hooks out of fishes' mouths.

To cope with all species and conditions you'll need an array of rods, from an ultra-light 8lb class for small fish inshore to an 80lb class for offshore monsters.

Choosing Your Rod

1 Light-actioned rods can handle decent-sized fish and provide a lot of fun.

2 The 15lb-class Ugly Stik is a popular rod for targeting cod and rays inshore, or for fishing shads for pollack on offshore wrecks.

3 Fishing for blonde rays on offshore banks or rough ground for congers will require a rod with a bit more power, like this 30lb-class rod.

4 Uptiding rods are longer to enable you to cast further.

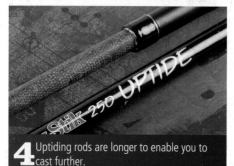

5 Look for a rod with a supple tip that will tire a fish but not tear the hook out during the fight.

6 A few boat rods have two or three tips or fibreglass push-in tips for better bite detection.